MARCEL BREUER: Furniture and Interiors

D1561272

MARCEL BREUER
Furniture and Interiors

by Christopher Wilk

Introduction by
J. Stewart Johnson

The Museum of Modern Art
New York

The exhibition "Marcel Breuer: Furniture and Interiors" has been generously supported by SCM Corporation and organized with the aid of a grant from the National Endowment for the Arts.

Copyright © 1981 by The Museum of Modern Art
All rights reserved
Library of Congress Catalog Card Number 81–81191
Clothbound ISBN 0-87070-264-5
Paperbound ISBN 0-87070-263-7
Designed by Nora Sheehan
Typeset by M. J. Baumwell Typography, Inc.,
    New York, N.Y.
Printed by Halliday Lithograph Corp.,
    West Hanover, Mass.
Bound by Sendor Bindery, Inc., New York, N.Y.
The Museum of Modern Art
11 West 53 Street, New York, N.Y. 10019
Printed in the United States of America

Frontispiece: Marcel Breuer supervising construction of the Harnismacher house, Wiesbaden, 1932.

Contents

ACKNOWLEDGMENTS

Marcel Breuer: Furniture and Interiors is published in conjunction with the exhibition of the same name presented at The Museum of Modern Art. This is the third in a series of five exhibitions devoted to twentieth-century designers whose work has had a profound effect on design in our time. The Marcel Breuer exhibition was preceded by those on Charles Eames (1973) and Ludwig Mies van der Rohe (1977) and will be followed by ones on Alvar Aalto and Le Corbusier.

The works in the previous exhibitions were drawn almost entirely from The Museum of Modern Art's own Design Collection. In the case of Marcel Breuer, however, despite the Museum's important holdings of Breuer material, so long and varied was his career in designing furniture that the sixteen Breuer pieces from the Museum's collection on view have had to be supplemented by extensive loans, both European and American, institutional and private. In addition, one important design known only through photographs has been reconstructed by the Museum with the designer's participation.

This book has benefited from the generous cooperation of Marcel Breuer. His kindness and good humor during repeated interviews not only contributed a great deal toward a reconstruction of his career, but also made my work enjoyable. My deepest appreciation extends also to his wife, Constance Breuer, who showed untiring patience in answering my questions.

Jack Pritchard provided invaluable assistance through his recollections of early modernism in England and through his comments on my first draft of the Isokon section. His continuing enthusiastic interest in Isokon, as well as in Breuer's work, was more than I could have asked for.

Ise Gropius was ever willing to discuss Breuer and the Bauhaus, as well as the many decades of close friendship between her husband, herself, and Breuer. She was kind enough to provide me with excerpts from the diary (soon to be published) of her Bauhaus years. I was fortunate also to be able to speak with former Bauhaus student Andrew Weininger, a native of Breuer's birthplace; his wife Eva, who was a student in the Bauhaus carpentry workshop; and the late Nina Kandinsky—all of whom knew Breuer well during his Bauhaus years.

I owe special thanks to Nina Bremer, whose comments on the manuscript brought to my attention many details of Breuer's career that I was not aware of. Peter Blake was kind enough to discuss various points concerning Breuer as well as the circumstances surrounding the writing of his 1949 monograph, which remains the launching point for any consideration of Breuer's career.

A number of Breuer's former students, associates, and clients were kind enough to share with me their recollections of Breuer and his work. In particular I wish to extend warmest thanks to Edward L. Barnes, Herbert Bayer, Laurence Curry, Alan I W Frank, Dorothy Gane, Bert Geller, Gertrud Lewin, Christian Nordmann, Leopold Reidemeister, Dahlan K. Ritchey, and Richard Stein.

I am greatly indebted to the individuals and institutions that assisted in the locating of Breuer-designed objects (many of which were generously lent to the exhibition that this monograph accompanies). My benefactors in this respect include Manfred Ludewig, Berlin; Dr. Hans Wingler, Dr. Peter Hahn, and Dr. Christian Wolsdorff, Bauhaus Archiv, Berlin; Dr. L. Honigmann-Zinserling, Staatliches Kunstsammlung, Weimar; Cleo Witt, City Museum and Art Gallery, Bristol; Charles Newton and Leela Meinertas, Victoria and Albert Museum; Suzanne Spain, Bryn Mawr College; Kevin Stayton and Dianne Pilgrim, The Brooklyn

Museum; Professor Andreas Giedion, Zurich; Ken Stradling, The Bristol Guild; Christine Bevington, New York; and the Drawings Collection of the Royal Institute of British Architects.

The staffs of various institutions, as well as several individuals and companies, provided assistance with research. I gratefully acknowledge the help of Carolyn A. Davis, George Arents Research Library, Syracuse University; Cheryl Buckley, University of Newcastle-upon-Tyne; Emilie Dana and Winfried Nerdinger, Busch-Reisinger Museum, Harvard University; Joan Burgasser of Thonet Industries, York, Pennsylvania; and Georg Thonet of Gebrüder Thonet, Frankenberg, West Germany. I owe a special debt of gratitude to Peter Fletcher, who not only allowed me to spend several days studying the papers of his former partner, Anton Lorenz, but also greatly added to my knowledge of Lorenz and of inventors in general through several fascinating discussions.

Special thanks are due to Lily Auchincloss for her interest in and support of this book, and the exhibition it accompanies, during the preliminary stages of research. I owe thanks to Ludwig Glaeser for his encouragement and assistance during the early stages of this project; the same appreciation is extended to Rosemarie Bletter of Columbia University. For assistance in various matters of research I must express my appreciation to Jessica Rutherford, Brighton Art Gallery and Museum; Roger Huntley, London; and Karl Rössing, Marchtrenk, Upper Austria. I am grateful for cooperation extended to me by Marcel Breuer Associates, especially by Herbert Beckhard, and by Howard Settles, who provided photographs. For assistance in locating negatives or providing new photography I must acknowledge the work of Richard Cheek, Reinhard Friedrich, S. M. Hind of the Architectural Press, and Erica Stoller of ESTO.

This book originated when I began working on the Design Collection of The Museum of Modern Art in 1976. For the opportunity to pursue the subject over the last several years I am especially grateful to Arthur Drexler, Director of the Department of Architecture and Design. J. Stewart Johnson, Curator of Design, not only encouraged the project but offered invaluable assistance through his painstaking criticism of the manuscript. His perceptive observations and knowledge of the period have proven invaluable and have immeasurably improved this book. I owe special thanks to Robert Coates for the many questions he raised concerning Breuer's furniture, as well as for his constant assistance. I was fortunate in being able to rely on the skill of Francis Kloeppel for the editing of the final manuscript. Other members of the Museum's staff who offered generous help include Mikki Carpenter, Marie-Anne Evans, Susan Evens, Tom Griesel, Christopher Holme, Kate Keller, Mary Jane Lightbown, Cara McCarty, Timothy McDonough, Mali Olatunji, Richard Palmer, Clive Phillpot, Charles Rodemeyer, Janette Rozene, Nora Sheehan, Mary Beth Smalley, and Richard Tooke.

Finally, I owe special debts of gratitude to Kathleen Fluegel, who translated voluminous correspondence, contracts, and difficult court decisions that greatly expanded my knowledge of Breuer's career; Steven Masket, who not only made all of the legal documents intelligible, but also managed to read and improve the first draft of this book; and Susan Harris, whose criticism and support have enormously contributed to the completion of this project.

CHRISTOPHER WILK

Introduction

The year 1925 was a watershed in the history of twentieth-century design because of two events: one public, spectacular, much heralded; the other private, though not unnoticed, and ultimately of more far-reaching significance. The first was the Exposition Internationale des Arts Décoratifs et Industriels in Paris, a monster rally for the decorative arts intended by its organizers to demonstrate conclusively that the French industries dedicated to the manufacture of *objets de luxe* had entirely recovered from the 1914–18 war's destruction of workshops and decimation of craftsmen. It served as a proclamation to the rest of the world that French taste and French workmanship were without rival, that Paris housed the spirit of modern design; Paris was its home.

The Exposition was vast, running from the Invalides down to the Seine, across the Pont Alexandre III (which was fitted up with lines of boutiques for the occasion), and stretching along the Right Bank from the Grand Palais to the Place de la Concorde. All the major nations displayed the furniture, glass, ceramics, metalwork, and textiles of which they were most proud—all, that is, but two. Germany was excluded; the war was too close, the bitterness of the French against their defeated enemy still too sharp. And America, which as one of France's principal allies was assigned a place of honor in the plan, looked at its invitation and at itself and regretfully declined, declaring itself hors de combat, admitting that it produced no modern design worth exhibiting.

For that was the catch and the key to the Exposition: *modern* design. Other World's Fairs, from London's 1851 Crystal Palace on, had allowed participants to display whatever wares they excelled in making, from goldsmiths' work to heavy machinery. Furniture might be designed in the latest fashion or more or less faithfully reproduce historic styles. In 1925, however, everything was required to be modern. In view of this decree, it is ironic that the style which the French touted as supremely modern and which most of their competitors conceded to be—although none of them felt as comfortable with it as did the French—was what later came to be known as Art Deco. And Art Deco, despite its occasional use of brilliant colors and eccentric forms, was essentially conservative, based on a neo-classicism that combined more often than not the weighty, symmetrical forms of Louis Philippe with the elegant surface decoration of Louis XVI— garlands of flowers, swags of drapery, nymphs, and graceful animals. It was aimed accurately at the haute bourgeoisie and the rich new industrialists, who could be expected to admire the quality of its workmanship and the opulence of its materials while being reassured by its references to a highly decorous past.

As it happened, the 1925 Exposition not only signaled the triumph of the Art Deco style, but also turned out to be its high-water mark. Art Deco would persist, though increasingly compromised, for fifteen years. From 1925 on, however, it rapidly lost ground to its rival style, modernism; and this was due largely to that second, private event of the year: Marcel Breuer's creation in Dessau of the first chair to be made out of bent steel tubes.

Modernism had existed prior to 1925. The modernists traced their roots back to the nineteenth century—to, in fact, Joseph Paxton's Crystal Palace, which had been built to house the first World's Fair and which they consid-

ered to be ''more of a direct ancestor of the new style than any one building of its time.''[1] More immediately, at the beginning of the twentieth century, their aesthetic and intellectual prejudices had been shaped largely by the industrial architecture of Peter Behrens (in whose office three of the leading modernist designers—Ludwig Mies van der Rohe, Walter Gropius, and Le Corbusier—worked as young men); by the architecture of Adolf Loos and, more particularly, his stern admonitions against the use of ornament; and by the ferroconcrete constructions of the brothers Perret. Emerging from this background, it is not surprising that the first explicitly modernist building in Europe was itself a factory: Walter Gropius' Fagus Shoe Works of 1911.

Holland's de Stijl, Russia's Constructivism, and Italy's Futurism were all powerful and related manifestations of the new aesthetic, but modernism did not really come into its own in architecture until the resumption of widespread building after the 1918 Armistice. Then avant-garde architects and designers all over Europe began to experiment with it. The single most widely recognized symbol of modernism, however, came to be the Bauhaus. It had been formed in Weimar shortly after the war as a trade school offering intensive instruction in art and the crafts; but by 1925, the year in which Walter Gropius built his quintessentially modernist structure to house the school in Dessau, it had shifted its emphasis from craft toward industry.

Marcel Breuer was a generation younger than the pioneers of the modernist movement, a child of the century. In 1925, when he designed his first tubular-steel chair, he was twenty-three; Gropius was forty-two, Mies thirty-nine, Oud thirty-five, and Le Corbusier thirty-eight. Breuer was a creature of the Bauhaus. He began his career as a student there and by 1925, as Gropius' protégé, had become Master of the furniture workshop. His early essays in furniture, not surprisingly, revealed close affinities to the ideas of de Stijl, particularly as they were articulated in the designs of Gerrit Rietveld, whose work was well known at the Bauhaus. Breuer, however, turned decisively away from these board-and-stick constructions when he got the idea of bending the metal tubes out of which his bicycle's handlebars were made into a structure that could support a seat and back and become a chair frame. The club chair that grew out of this idea was the first of a number of designs for tubular-steel furniture he made over the next six years, many of which were to become classics. But impressive as may be Breuer's individual designs, it is the idea behind them that assures him his place as the most influential designer of furniture in the twentieth century.

There seems to have been an instant recognition among architects and designers that bent tubular steel was the ideal material for modernist furniture. Photographs of Breuer's club chair were published even before he had a chance to fully work out its design, and as soon as the news got round, other designers seem to have decided that they too should try tubular steel, that they too should see what they could do with the material. It seemed to have everything. Furniture made of tubular steel was strong, lightweight, easily portable, and inexpensive to produce, since it required little of the handcraftmanship of conventional wood construction. And — in some ways even more appealing — it *looked* new; not only was it machine-made, it *looked* machine-made. The cool austerity, the sleek gleam of metal were exactly what had been needed to bring the modernist interior to life. Le Corbusier had followed his famous dictum in *Vers une Architecture* that "a house is a machine for living in" with the further thought that "a chair is a machine for sitting in." Here, unmistakably, was that machine.

In 1932, Alfred H. Barr, Jr., attempted to codify the principles and describe the characteristics of the new modernist architecture, which he dubbed "the International Style." In his foreword to the catalog of "Modern Architecture, International Exhibition," a show organized by Philip Johnson and Henry-Russell Hitchcock, Jr., for The Museum of Modern Art, Barr stated that "the aesthetic principles of the International Style are based primarily upon the nature of modern materials and structure," and went on to explain:

> Slender steel posts and beams, and concrete reinforced by steel have made possible structures of skeleton-like strength and lightness.

> …the modern architect working in the new style conceives of his building…as a skeleton enclosed by a thin light shell. He thinks in terms of *volume* — of space enclosed by planes or surfaces — as opposed to *mass* and solidity. This principle of volume leads him to make his walls seem thin flat surfaces by eliminating moldings and by making his windows and doors flush with the surface.

Barr pointed out that "both vertical and horizontal repetition and…flexible asymmetry" were "natural concomitants of modern buildings." "Positive quality or beauty in the International Style," he wrote,

> depends upon technically perfect use of materials whether metal, wood, glass or concrete; upon the fineness of proportions in units such as doors and windows and in the relationship between these units and the whole design. The negative or obverse aspect of this principle is the elimination of any kind of ornament or artificial pattern. This lack of ornament is one of the most difficult elements of the style for the layman to accept[2]

Barr was, of course, writing about modernist buildings, not about modernist interiors (except insofar as there was an implied consistency between a building's interior and exterior), and even less about modernist furniture. And yet the qualities he admired in modernist architecture could be applied almost as well to Breuer's first tubular-steel chair. It too was skeletal. Its form was dictated by the nature of the modern materials out of which it was constructed. Breuer's concern clearly was with volume—"space enclosed by planes or surfaces"—rather than mass. He vigorously avoided any ornament or pattern; the chair achieved its effect, in Barr's words, through "the clean perfection of surface and proportion."3

Photographs or drawings of the interiors of modernist buildings designed before 1925 are rare, and such photographs as exist usually show them devoid of furnishings. This may be because in their architects' haste to have them published, they were photographed before the paint was dry and the clients could move in their furniture. It may also be because the architects had not solved the problem of finding or designing consonant furnishings and preferred to have their interiors shown empty and pure, before they were spoiled by the impedimenta of living.

Take Mies, for example. Before 1925, his designs for modernist houses never progressed beyond the project stage. His drawings for them were widely published; but, although in later years he frequently produced evocative sketches of the interiors of his houses, none is known to exist from this period. It is a suggestive void and seems even more so when one considers that Mies began his career as a furniture designer before becoming an architect. The elegance of the steel-framed furniture he began to produce in 1927 and the lambent beauty of his interiors for the Barcelona Pavilion (1929) and Tugendhat house (1930) are unsurpassed. But they all follow Breuer's breakthrough.

Even more interesting is the case of Le Corbusier, who, in addition to designing highly influential buildings, acted as a proselytizer for modernism through his journal, *L'Esprit Nouveau*, and his books, especially the 1923 *Vers une Architecture*, which, soon translated into German and English, became a bible for the modernists. But despite abundant evidence that he was searching for new approaches to the problem of furnishing his interiors, his own solutions were at best tentative. Unlike Mies, Le Corbusier had already built several important houses by 1925; and in addition to photographs of these (the interiors of which were shown almost bare of furnishings), he published renderings of the interiors of numerous unexecuted projects. In these drawings, however, he relies upon a limited and for the most part conventional repertoire of furniture: overstuffed club chairs, grand pianos, simple dining tables, dining chairs that range from Thonet bentwood side chairs and armchairs to ladderback chairs and even neoclassical upholstered tub-back armchairs with sabre legs. On his terraces and roof gardens he places chairs and tables made of metal wire. Perhaps his most conservative creation is a large formal desk in his sketch of a "Monol" house; it could easily be mistaken for the work of Ruhlmann, Süe et Mare, Leleu, or any of the masters of the Art Deco style. His most innovative ideas concern storage systems; as early as 1915 he advocated the use of modular, mass-produced built-in storage units (although the symmetrical sideboards portrayed in his renderings of dining areas are typical of the more simple furniture widely available at the time).

In *Vers une Architecture*, Le Corbusier inveighed against "your bergères, your Louis XVI settees, bulging through their tapestry covers." "Are these machines for sitting in?" he asked. And yet the only chairs he specifically recommended are rush-seated church chairs, luxuriously upholstered armchairs, and Morris chairs "with a moveable reading-desk, a shelf for your coffee cup, an extending foot-rest, a back that raises and lowers with a handle, and gives you the very best positions either for work or a nap, in a healthy, comfortable, and right way."[4] This is all very well; but despite his hortatory tone, Morris chairs were hardly revolutionary in 1923. Elsewhere he wrote of the virtues of steamer trunks, metal office desks, and filing cabinets.

Curiously, Le Corbusier came close to Breuer's discovery. For years he flirted with the idea of mass-produced metal storage units, and his use of Thonet bentwood chairs and bent-wire garden chairs became almost a trademark. In 1925, when over the opposition of the organizers of the Exposition Internationale des Arts Décoratifs et Industriels he erected his uncompromisingly modernist Pavillon de l'Esprit Nouveau, he included in its furnishings handsome modular storage cabinets raised on metal pipes and tables with pipe legs. He even used bent metal tubes to form the handrail for his staircase. But he did not recognize the potential of the material. Subsequently, he looked back and claimed with characteristic hubris that "the Pavillon de l'Esprit Nouveau was a turning point in the design of modern interiors and a milestone in the evolution of architecture."[5]

He was right in part: the importance of the Pavillon as architecture cannot be challenged, particularly in view of its exceptional role in the Exposition as a paradigm of modernism, standing out against an almost entirely Art Deco agglomeration. But "a turning point in the design of modern interiors"? Hardly. The interiors of the Pavillon de l'Esprit Nouveau are disappointing. The storage cabinets are very fine, as are such accouterments as the Léger painting and the model airplane mounted on the wall. But the movable furniture, the chairs, are neither new nor unexpected.

In 1927, Le Corbusier (together with Pierre Jeanneret and Charlotte Perriand) would begin to design chairs made of tubular steel; but in 1925, he still had not seen the way. In *Vers une Architecture*, he wrote:

> Our epoch is fixing its own style day by day. It is here under our eyes.
> Eyes which do not see[6]

It was Marcel Breuer, working in Dessau, who did see and whose imagination made possible the full realization of the modernist interior. His 1925 design set off a tremendous burst of creativity around him. He himself, after designing a number of furniture forms in tubular steel, went on to experiment with other materials: aluminum, plywood, and, toward the end of his career, monumental sculptural shapes in stone and bushhammered concrete (in which his early subtle manipulation of volume was replaced by an affirmation of mass). But had he accomplished nothing beyond that first tubular-steel chair, his signal importance would remain for his vision of a new kind of furniture, the machine for sitting in, the chair within the handlebars.

J. STEWART JOHNSON
Curator of Design
Department of Architecture and Design
The Museum of Modern Art

Notes

1. Philip Johnson, "Historical Note," in Henry-Russell Hitchcock, Jr., Philip Johnson, et al., *Modern Architecture, International Exhibition* (New York: MoMA, 1932), p. 19.
2. Hitchcock, Johnson, et al., op. cit., pp. 14-15.
3. Ibid., p. 15.
4. Le Corbusier, *Towards a New Architecture*, tr. from 13th French ed. by Frederick Etchells (London: John Rodker, 1927), p. 119.
5. Le Corbusier, *Le Corbusier et Pierre Jeanneret, Oeuvre Complète, 1910-1929* (Zurich: Les Editions d'Architecture, 1964), p. 104.
6. Le Corbusier, *Towards a New Architecture*, p. 95.

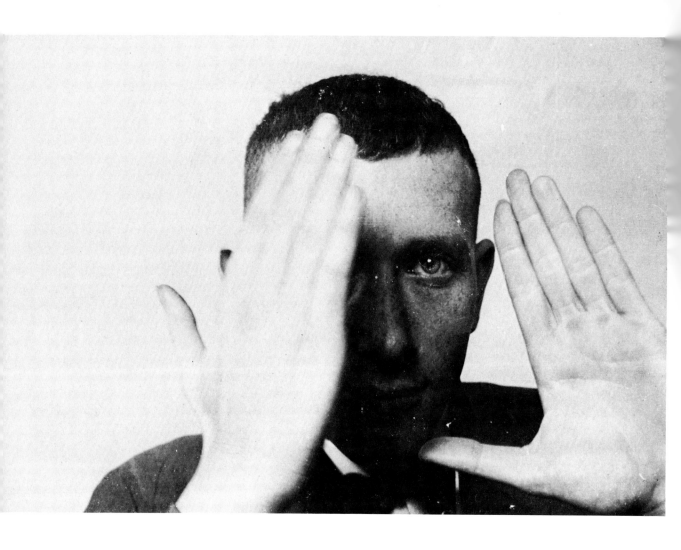

**Marcel Breuer at the Dessau Bauhaus during
the mid-1920s.**

Youth and Early Work
1902–25

Marcel Lajos Breuer was born on 22 May 1902, in Pécs, in southwestern Hungary.[1] A city of 42,000 inhabitants, Pécs was a center of mining and industry in an essentially agricultural country. After the fall of the Hapsburgs at the end of the First World War and the dissolution of the Austro-Hungarian Empire, it became one of five major provincial centers of the new Hungarian Republic. Throughout Breuer's childhood and youth, however, it was already the economic and cultural center of virtually all of western Hungary, a progressive and intellectual city with a university.

Jacob Breuer, Marcel's father, was a dental technician, an educated man who was able to support his wife and children in a comfortable middle-class way of life. Although both parents were Jewish, Breuer rejected religion at a young age.[2] His parents encouraged their children to take an active interest in culture and the arts, and toward that end they subscribed to art periodicals, among them *The Studio* magazine (although no one in the house read or spoke English), which, though published in London, was widely read on the Continent for its coverage of current developments in applied and fine arts and architecture. Within this background Breuer decided that he would become an artist: a painter, or perhaps a sculptor. In 1920, at the age of eighteen, he obtained a scholarship to the Fine Arts Academy (Akademie der bildenden Künste) in Vienna.

Beyond these scanty details, little is known about Breuer's youth in Hungary. Breuer himself has always regarded details about his life as completely irrelevant to any discussion of his work. He has therefore, except in private company, been extremely reticent about providing facts that could give a more coherent account of his youth, or of later periods in his life.

Breuer must have left for Vienna with high expectations. Despite the ravages of the First World War and the general instability of the new Austrian Republic, Vienna was still one of the great cultural centers of the world. The aspiring artist, however, lasted only a matter of hours at the Academy. He found the classes, and students, more occupied with lengthy, pretentious discussions about aesthetic theory than with learning the fundamentals of drawing, painting, and sculpting, and he walked out. Faced with the loss of his scholarship and anxious for "practical" training, he took a job in a local architect's office. Here he remained longer: a matter of weeks rather than hours. Breuer then left to move north to Weimar, Germany, where, he had been told by his friend Fred Forbat (another native of Pécs, who had recently obtained his architectural degree), a new kind of art school had recently been founded[3] It was called the Bauhaus.

Marcel Breuer entered the Bauhaus in Weimar in 1920 as a student. He graduated in 1924, left briefly to live and work in Paris, but returned in 1925 to become head of the carpentry workshop, remaining until 1928, when he left for good. His education at the Bauhaus was of such critical importance to his art that it is impossible to consider his work without also discussing the institution itself.

Breuer was among the very first of a group of young painters, architects, and designers whose artistic identities were molded by the Bauhaus. If he had many preconceived notions about art and design when he arrived, it is safe to assume they were profoundly transformed after a brief time at the new school. His receptivity to new ideas and his apparent dislike for traditional art education favored his development at this unusual institution. He was there almost at the beginning, and he participated in, and contributed to, the many crucial changes that occurred during the early years of the school. And his work, perhaps more than that of any other student, reflected the change in philosophy of the Bauhaus from the primarily craft orientation with which it began, to the principles of the merging of art and industry for which it subsequently became famous.

From the beginning he was singled out as an outstanding student. He gradually became a close friend of Walter and Ise Gropius, the school's Director and his wife. And for nearly two decades, from 1920 to 1940, Breuer's professional life was largely shaped by his friendship with Walter Gropius, and by Gropius' respect for Breuer as an artist and designer.

A description of the eighteen-year-old Breuer was provided almost thirty years later by Gropius:

> . . . in those years [Breuer was] the prototype of a very intelligent, sophisticated cosmopolitan with Bohemian or urban characteristics. It would have been very difficult at that time to tell from which background he came. There were certainly no middle-class or small-town leanings in him. On the contrary, he was remarkably free of any such ties when he entered the Bauhaus as a young man[4]

WALTER GROPIUS AND THE BAUHAUS WEIMAR

When Breuer arrived in Weimar in 1920, the Bauhaus was barely a year old. In April of 1919, Walter Gropius had become director of the Staatliches Bauhaus Weimar, an institution created to replace the Grand Ducal Arts and Crafts School and the Grand Ducal Fine Arts Academy. The Bauhaus was largely the product of Gropius' own conception of art and design education, and reflected his ideas from the preceding decade.

In 1915, after the beginning of the First World War, Henry van de Velde, a Belgian architect of international renown who was the director of the Arts and Crafts School, was forced to resign because he was a foreigner. Among the three individuals he recommended as possible successors was Gropius, whom he seemed to regard as the best choice. Gropius' architectural work, including the startlingly modern Fagus factory (1911) and the administration building for the 1914 Deutscher Werkbund exhibition, was well known to van de Velde. The Werkbund, of which van de Velde was a founder, was an organization of artists (mostly architects), businessmen, and teachers that had been established to promote a close relationship between art and industry and improve the quality of German design.

In the Werkbund Yearbook of 1913, Gropius had written about the important relationship that needed to be forged between the artist and industry:

> The artist has the power to give the lifeless machine-made product a soul. His collaboration is...an indispensable part of the industrial process and must be regarded as such[5]

had fostered, between the Arts and Crafts School and the local craft industry, a working relationship that led to "business transactions"; after van de Velde's departure supervising authorities felt that this relationship should be "retained by all means and expanded."[6] But in October of 1915, with the escalation of the war, the Grand Duke disbanded the Arts and Crafts School and turned its building into a military hospital. Nevertheless, while he was in the army, Gropius continued his discussions with the Interior Ministry (to whose jurisdiction the Grand Ducal schools had shifted) about his possible role in a new applied art and architecture department which the Ministry hoped to add to the Fine Arts Academy. Gropius disagreed with the proposal and wrote that "the teaching of architecture...is all-encompassing...[and requires] an autonomous teaching organization."[7] Pressed by the Ministry to explain the role of art and craft in such a scheme, Gropius drew from his earlier writings and answered by showing the relationship between craft, machine production, and the artist:

> The manufacturer must see to it that he adds the noble quality of handmade objects to the advantages of mechanical production. Only then will the original idea of industry—a substitute for handwork by mechanical means—find its complete realization....
>
> The artist posesses the ability to breathe soul into the lifeless product of the machine ...His collaboration is not a luxury, not a pleasing adjunct; it must become an indispensable component in the total output of modern industry...

He concluded his memo with a reference to the medieval craft tradition, which had little to do with the emphasis on machine production, but which prefigured Gropius' idea of the Bauhaus as a community of artist-craftsmen:

Errata:

Page 17, bottom column 1: Add:
  Gropius' advocacy of these views made him a particularly impressive candidate for the job in van de Velde's eyes. Van de Velde

Passim:
For "Harnismacher" read "Harnischmacher"

Among its participants a similarly happy partnership might re-emerge as that practiced in the medieval "lodges," where numerous related artist-craftsmen...came together in a homogeneous spirit and humbly contributed their independent work to common taste.[8]

Gropius had fought in the war from 1914 until 1918, when he was wounded and sent back to Berlin. Like much of Europe's intellectual community, he was appalled by the slaughter and destruction caused by the war. After the November Revolution in Germany, which led to the abdication of the Kaiser, Gropius helped found, and later became chairman of, the revolutionary Arbeitsrat für Kunst (Working Council for Art). Through this group, Gropius codified many of the principles that would become important at the Bauhaus and began correspondence with the new government to see if he was still being considered for a post at the Weimar Art Academy. In January of 1919 his appointment as director of the Art Academy and also of the Arts and Crafts School was confirmed. Following his request, the name of the newly combined school was changed to Staatliches Bauhaus Weimar, and in April Gropius assumed the post of director. The official Program for the new school, written by Gropius, was the document that had led to Breuer's departure from Vienna. Fed up with the refined aestheticism of Viennese art circles and interested in the practical "making" of objects, Breuer was moved by Gropius' powerful exhortation, which read, in part:

> The ultimate aim of all visual arts is the complete building!...Architects, painters, and sculptors must recognize anew and learn to grasp the composite character of a building both as an entity and in its composite parts....
>
> Architects, sculptors, painters, we must all return to the crafts! For art is not a "profession." There is no essential difference between the artist and the craftsman. The artist is an exalted craftsman. In rare mo-

ments of inspiration, transcending the consciousness of his will, the grace of heaven may cause his work to blossom into art. But proficiency in a craft is essential to every artist! Therein lies the prime source of creative imagination. Let us then create a new guild of craftsmen without class distinctions that raise an arrogant barrier between craftsman and artist! Together let us desire, conceive, and create the new structure, which will embrace architecture and sculpture and painting in one unity and which one day will rise toward heaven from the hands of a million workers like the crystal symbol of the new faith.[9]

In this first manifesto of the Bauhaus, the emphasis was placed squarely on the learning and mastery of craft. Gropius made no mention of the machine or of technology. The aim of the early Bauhaus was to train architects, painters, and sculptors as craftsmen; "art" could only be achieved through the mastery of craft. The school would nurture "a new guild of craftsmen" who would build the structures of the future. The primarily craft orientation of the Program was surely a reflection of the Ministry's wish that the school fulfill practical needs and that it continue to develop the relationship with the local craft industry. The highly romanticized tone and the references to the medieval guild reflected a romanticism and utopianism in Gropius' thinking that had appeared only with the cataclysmic upheaval of the war and through the influence of expressionist artists, including the members of the Blaue Reiter (the painters Marc, Kandinsky, and Klee) and those associated with the magazine *Der Sturm* (the architects Bruno Taut, Adolf Behne, and even Adolf Loos).[10]

Education for the new craftsmen would begin with an introductory course of six months, which was intended to familiarize the students with the basic principles, material, and processes of all the visual arts, and the ultimate aim of which was to teach the students

Fig. 1. "African" chair, wood with woven uphol-   19
stery, 1921. Breuer's first known student work
reflected the earlier romantic or expressionist period of the Bauhaus.

"the language of creativity" and allow their natural talent to find expression.[11] After the introduction the students would move into one of several workshops where they would work under the guidance of a Master of Craft, from whom they would learn basic technique, and a Master of Form, who would deal with problems of form and content.

According to his own account, Breuer arrived too late in the term to join the introductory course.[12] He looked into several different courses and settled on the carpentry or woodworking workshop, where he finally received the "practical" training he had sought in Vienna.

Walter Gropius envisioned Bauhaus workshops for all materials: stone, wood, metal, clay, glass, color (wall painting), and textiles. Drawing and painting were required but taught separately. When Breuer arrived in Weimar, however, the only fully equipped workshops were those in weaving and bookbinding. The severe economic problems in Germany forced the school to wait several years before obtaining the funds necessary for full operation, and the other workshops, when they were opened in 1920, had only enough equipment to allow them to be run on a limited basis.

In 1921, the wood or carpentry workshop was directed by Form Master Johannes Itten, one of the most charismatic and controversial of the original Bauhaus masters, who also taught the introductory course, and Craft Master Joseph Zachmann. Under their guidance Breuer began to develop his knowledge of wood and his own sense of design.

WOODEN FURNITURE (I)

Breuer's earliest known design (fig. 1), the so-called "African chair" of 1921, was an unusual work, even for the early Bauhaus. The high-backed five-legged chair was upholstered with brightly colored and boldly patterned fabric. Even the wooden frame was decorated with colored horizontal striping. The chair is said to have been "roughly hewn" with an ax; the wooden parts were left unplaned.[13] The design suggests the work of a student responding to a variety of influences; the Magyar folk art of Breuer's native Hungary, the vogue for African art in Europe, and the interest in naive art and the occult encouraged by Itten must all have played a part in its conception. The design of the chair, with its upholstered seat and back (presumably woven in the Bauhaus textile workshop), its decorated frame elements, and the unusual crossing of the two side pieces at the top of the back, made the chair seem more suitable for an African potentate than for a European of the 1920s.

Far more restrained and conventional was a slightly later side chair of 1921 (fig. 2), the

Fig. 2. Side chair, ebonized wood with woven upholstery, 1921. (Collection Staatliches Kunstsammlung, Weimar.) Upholstered with Gunta Stölzl's multicolored wool strips, the chair was characterized by a simplified geometry that became prevalent in Breuer's work.

brightly colored upholstered seat and back of which were woven by the leading student of the textile workshop, Gunta Stölzl. Its more economical and angular treatment still betrayed the influence of the primitive in its design and construction. The stavelike pieces which formed the front legs and rear stiles tapered in from top to bottom, gently but noticeably. And most important, they were attached to the seat and back frames in a manner that accentuated their separateness or independence from the seat and back. This separateness, which included their rising above the seat and back, asserted the chair's references to African primitive and European country or folk furniture. The design, according to Breuer, elicited the qualified approval of Theo van Doesburg, founder of the Dutch de Stijl group; during a visit to the Bauhaus, he found fault only with the curve of the back.

A chair and table of quite a different order were designed in 1921 for the Sommerfeld house of 1920–21[14] (fig. 3), the first collaborative effort of the Bauhaus workshops for an actual building. The house for the timber industrialist Adolf Sommerfeld in Berlin provided the first opportunity for the school to realize its aim, as enunciated by Gropius, of snythesizing art and craft to "create the new structure, which will embrace architecture and sculpture and painting in one unity…" It was also the strongest manifestation of the romantic and utopian ideas which Gropius had adopted during the war. The Sommerfeld house was a remarkable building that lived up to the standards set for the Bauhaus by its director at its inception. And its clearly expressionist character seemed to contradict his earlier belief in a precise, industrially oriented art.

Gropius and his architectural partner Adolf Meyer were awarded the commission by Sommerfeld; they, in turn, involved the Bauhaus workshops. Unusual as it was to construct a house during such depressed times, even more unusual was the fact that the house was made entirely from teak, salvaged from the interior of a ship. The entrance hall was a tour de force, startling in its originality and its angular, geometrical expressionism. This was due, in large part, to the expressive but carefully controlled work of Joost Schmidt, a gifted student, and Schmidt's colleagues in the sculpture workshop.

The heavy upholstered armchair (fig. 4) designed by Breuer for use in the entrance hall (unfortunately photographs of other rooms do not survive) stood in marked contrast to the design of the interior itself. The many diagonal lines which served as a backdrop for the chairs provided a foil for their simplified geometry of right angles and rectangular shapes. Breuer's chair, said to have been executed in cherry wood and leather, was massive and cubelike in form. The bulky upholstered seat and back were carried on four legs, the rear legs extending up to support the back.

The chair was so different from Breuer's other chairs of 1921 (and so much more interesting) that one must wonder whether he independently developed the design or whether the Sommerfeld furniture reflected the ideas of another designer, perhaps Gropius. Comparison of the Sommerfeld chair with Gropius' cubelike office armchair of 1923 (fig. 5) suggests that it was the younger Breuer who was beginning to influence his teacher and friend.

The Breuer chair was reminiscent of certain cube chairs produced in Vienna and Darmstadt during the first decade of the century. But unlike those completely forward-looking designs, the cube form was, in the Breuer chair, tempered and enlivened by a lingering feeling for primitive folk furniture. This tendency is demonstrated in the extension of the front and rear legs above the seat and back and the emphatically separate articulation of the legs, which both literally and figuratively "carry" the bulk of the chair.

Fig. 3. Walter Gropius and Adolf Meyer, Sommerfeld house, Berlin-Dahlem, 1920. The
entrance hall, like the entire project, was
designed and executed with the collaboration of the Bauhaus workshops; construction
was completed in 1921.

Fig. 4. Armchair, cherry wood and leather, 22
Sommerfeld house, 1921. In the tradition of
early-twentieth-century "cube" chairs, the
armchair indicated the beginnings of the
de Stijl influence in Breuer's work.

The same might also be said of the simple round tea table (fig. 6), also executed for the Sommerfeld house in cherry wood. The thick circular table top was carried on five rectangular legs which also rose above the top of the surface being supported. The result was an abstract, sculptural composition of circle and volumetric rectangles.

By the time of the Sommerfeld designs, the urge toward geometrical simplification and abstraction and the emphasis on the separate geometrical components of each piece of furniture had become an important part of Breuer's work. This may, in part, have been the result of the increasing influence of an international constructivism, which through Dutch de Stijl and Russian Constructivism had made itself felt at the Bauhaus almost since its inception.

THE QUESTION OF DE STIJL INFLUENCE

Bauhaus Masters and students were very sensitive to most of the important European artistic currents of the period, and it is beyond question that they were well aware of the de Stijl group. The painter and Bauhaus master Lyonel Feininger, beginning in 1919, had introduced the work of de Stijl to those not already aware of it. He saw de Stijl as offering an alternative to "the heightened romanticism of many."[15] The furniture of the Dutch designer Gerrit Rietveld (figs. 8 and 9) was published in the journal De Stijl, among others, in 1919 and 1920. Theo van Doesburg himself, whose influence Gropius later decried but whose book the Bauhaus published in 1924, visited the school on several occasions beginning in 1921. Finally, Rietveld exhibited his furniture at the Bauhaus exhibition of 1923.

Despite the contact of de Stijl with the Bauhaus, a number of former teachers or students—or, as they became known, Bauhäusler—were adamant in their contention

Fig. 5. Walter Gropius, armchair, cherry wood with lemon-yellow upholstery, 1923, for the Bauhaus Director's office, Weimar. Gropius' design bears a close resemblance to Breuer's Sommerfeld chair.

Fig. 6. Tea table, cherry wood, 1921, also designed for the Sommerfeld house. The emphasis on "constructed" form characterized most of Breuer's work until 1926; the treatment of the round top and separately articulated legs recalls his "African" chair.

23

Fig. 7. Armchair, oak with orange upholstery, 1922. (Collection The Museum of Modern Art, Phyllis B. Lambert Fund.) Made in several different versions and in different woods, Breuer's design unquestionably reflected the influence of Rietveld's furniture. The upholstery was woven in the Bauhaus weaving workshop.

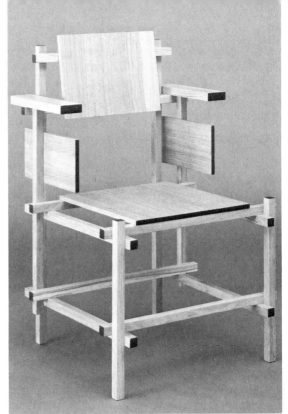

that the influence of de Stijl and van Doesburg was not important to the school. Van Doesburg and Gropius came to regard each other with considerable antipathy. Van Doesburg believed that he was personally responsible for the shift in the "creative mentality" of the students away from the earlier romantic expressionism to the rationalism of the school after 1923. "The intervention of de Stijl," he said, "brought the young artists back to order and discipline."[16] When these assertions were denied by the Bauhäusler, van Doesburg began to exhibit antagonistic and paranoid behavior toward the school, and toward Gropius especially. After learning that Rietveld had exhibited at the Bauhaus exhibition of 1923, van Doesburg wrote to his colleague:

> I was stunned to see...that you had joined in the Exposition of the Bauhaus in Weimar, thus working *against de Stijl.* That Wils and Oud joined does not surprise me very much; they are constantly advertising themselves.

But what advantage can you see in exhibiting *there.* I feel very miserable and realize that I must now give up the de Stijl idea because I am gradually, due to encircling intrigues, standing alone. This entire Bauhaus display results from the struggle which I had there; the exposition is intended as an immediate revenge against my influence and against my person. Gropius, the director, will use this demonstration only as a *raison d'être* for the Bauhaus and as a means of perpetuating it![17]

Gropius and others (including Breuer) felt that van Doesburg was grossly overstating his impact on the school. They argued that tendencies "parallel" to de Stijl and other constructivist groups had developed independently at the Bauhaus. Le Corbusier's writings on primary forms were cited as a more important influence.[18]

For some designers it may well have been true that their own personal development led

Fig. 8. Gerrit Rietveld, Red-Blue Chair, 1917–18. (Collection The Museum of Modern Art, gift of Philip Johnson.) Rietveld's famous chair was designed before he officially became a member of the de Stijl group, although it bore distinct affinities to the designs of Theo van Doesburg and the paintings of Piet Mondrian.

Fig. 9. Gerrit Rietveld, highback chair, wood, 1919. (Replica based on the original model; collection The Museum of Modern Art, gift of Cassina.) An elaborate de Stijl construction, this chair was published in 1920 and shown at the Bauhaus exhibition in Weimar in 1923.

them to artistic statements that paralleled those of de Stijl. It is also true that the influence of Russian and East European Constructivism played a role, although in the case of furniture design this role is difficult to define with precision. As for Breuer, however, the de Stijl influence on his furniture is too strong and too specific to be denied. All of his known furniture from 1921 until 1925 showed the clear and unmistakable influence of de Stijl, particularly of Rietveld's furniture, which played a singularly important role in Breuer's art.

WOODEN FURNITURE (II)

In 1922, the constructivist aesthetic implicit in Breuer's Sommerfeld house furniture emerged full-blown in an important armchair (fig. 7), several versions of which were made in the Bauhaus woodworking shop. (In this same year Gropius became Form Master of the shop, replacing Itten, and Reinhold Weidensee became Crafts Master. Both men would retain those positions until Breuer took over in 1925.)

Without precedent at the Bauhaus, the chair is a carefully composed series of planar elements floating in space. It is a neo–de Stijl construction very much related to the chairs of Gerrit Rietveld. In particular it calls to mind the so-called Highback chair of 1919 (fig. 9). Like the Rietveld chair, it declares itself as more than a simple chair to sit on. Pieces of the frame set at perpendicular angles pass through one another. The entire chair seems to cant back from the front legs. The arms and back hover in space. There is a tension between the apparent precariousness of the design and the obvious strength of the materials and construction.

Although the Breuer armchair can accept a person in comfort, it does not allow the sitter to violate or alter the essential structure of the chair. Rietveld's chair, on the other hand, neither invites sitting nor provides a comfortable seat and back for doing so. Breuer carefully differentiates between the soft spans of material that form part of the overall composition of the chair, and the hard wooden components of the elaborate structural frame. This is a characteristic that remains a constant in Breuer's chair designs, with only a very few exceptions.

This Breuer armchair in particular has a certain anthropomorphic appearance. There is an articulation of the legs, arms, and frame of the chair that mimics the seated human form.

What becomes of some interest in the 1922 chair is the structural principle of the cantilever, that is, the projection of a given element beyond its support. This is expressed in the extension of the arms above the seat and in the extension backward of the side frame pieces carrying the rear portion of the back. The can-

Fig. 10. Armchair, wood with upholstered seat and back rest, 1922. Breuer is said to have been the first person at the Bauhaus to use readymade plywood in his furniture instead of making it himself in the traditional practice of cabinetmakers, which persisted even into the 1930s and '40s.

tilevering of chair parts becomes more prevalent in Breuer's work in 1923 and seems to have held a fascination for him, as it did for other architects and designers of the period.

Another armchair (fig. 10), also of 1922, was surely designed under the influence of Rietveld's chairs. In it most of the structural elements were thinner and wider, including the seat, back, arms, and arm supports. The flatness of the various elements became part of the chair's aesthetic. Breuer again chose not to make the chair with a spare Rietveld-type of wood seat and back, and instead added cushions to both. These concessions to comfort, especially the back cushion, added not only to the chair's functional aspects but also to the variety of shape in the design.

A simple side chair design (fig. 11), executed in the following year in both children's and adult sizes, shared the same basic formal and structural characteristics as the 1922 chairs. Although the design varied slightly in different-size models of the chair, it remained essentially a simplified version of the earlier armchair with padded seat and headrest (fig. 10). In the later side chair, the back frame was reduced to a simple rectangular unit. Single pieces of plywood were used for both seat and back. Like most of the early wooden chairs, however, the side chairs seemed more like manifestos of a certain artistic sensibility than carefully considered chairs designed for comfortable sitting.

THE BAUHAUS EXHIBITION, 1923

By late 1922, Breuer, along with much of the Bauhaus community, was beginning to work

Fig. 11. Children's chairs and tables, plywood painted gray (table and chair seats and backs) and red (chair frames), 1922; rug designed by Benita Otte of the Bauhaus weaving workshop. The chairs were completely de Stijl, while the simple cube table was a more original and far more influential design, the inspiration for the so-called Parsons table.

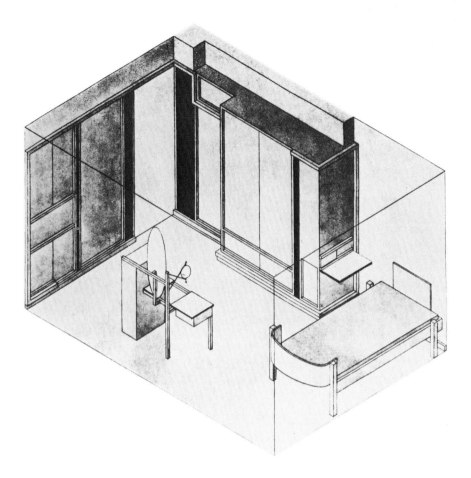

on projects for the first Bauhaus exhibition. Held at the insistence of the Thuringian government, under whose jurisdiction the school now fell, the exhibition was to be a summary of the first four years of the school's activities. Although Gropius and others felt that the time was not yet right for such a retrospective view, the pressure from the government and the press was such that it could not be delayed. Opponents of the school especially wanted to see what kinds of nonsense were being taught and produced, and they undoubtedly felt that the show would lead to the demise of the Bauhaus.

The exhibition involved displays by all of the workshops: an experimental single-family house designed by the painter Georg Muche, who was Form Master of the weaving work-

shop, and furnished by students and teachers, which was to be part of a projected housing development; an exhibition of architectural models, drawings, and photographs by a large group of international architects including Gropius, Mendelsohn, Poelzig, Stam, Scharoun, Le Corbusier, Oud, Rietveld, Wils, Wright, and several less-known Czechoslovak and Russian architects; a performance of Oskar Schlemmer's *Triadic Ballet*; and finally, a week of activities in August which included lectures by Gropius, Kandinsky, and Oud and music by Stravinsky, Hindemith, and Busoni. Breuer's work was exhibited with that of the carpentry workshop and in the experimental house, the Haus-am-Horn.

Six young Bauhaus designers were given the task of designing the rooms of the experi-

Fig. 12. Axonometric drawing, Room for a Woman, experimental Haus-am-Horn, Bauhaus exhibition, 1923. Breuer designed all of the furniture in the room, including the large wall unit with night table and the unusual walnut and lemon-wood vanity, the top of which slid horizontally along the length of the supporting frame.

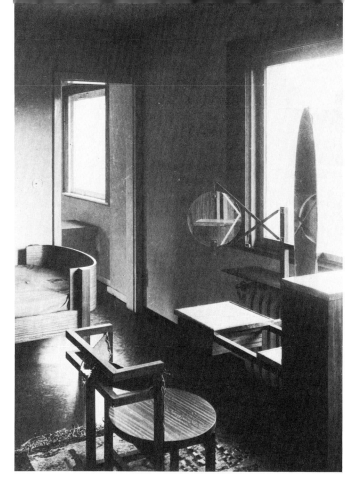

articulated. The wall unit was built into the wall under a large beam which projected from the ceiling. It contained a large double-doored space and narrower storage spaces to the right and left. Extended from the side of the unit, over the bed, was a night table, possibly collapsible.

For the centrally located living room with high ceiling and clerestory windows, Breuer provided a number of pieces in addition to his 1922 armchair, which was used throughout. He designed, and the cabinetmaking workshop produced, a simple free-standing, glass-fronted bookcase, a massive gray maple desk (fig. 14), and a large corner cabinet (fig. 15). The massing of the various parts of the large cabinet gave the unit a sculptural appearance that became typical of Bauhaus furniture by other designers in 1923–24.

The 1923 Bauhaus exhibition marked a turning point in the official policy of the school. As enunciated in Gropius' speech, "Art and Technology: The New Unity," which he gave during Bauhaus Week activities, and in his simultaneously published book, *The Theory and Organization of the Weimar Bauhaus*, the orientation of the school was to be more in the direction of industrial production. Although the teaching of craft would remain essential and important, Gropius wrote, "it is by no means an end in itself….The Bauhaus believes the machine to be our modern medium of design and seeks to come to terms with it."[20]

mental house. Their work was to reflect "New living problems, new technologies, arrangement and interior fittings."[19] Breuer designed the interiors of the woman's bedroom and the living room.

For the bedroom (figs. 12, 13) Breuer designed a vanity with chair, a bed, and a large wall unit, known only in an axonometric drawing of the room. The vanity and chair were complicated sculptural constructions, the frameworks of which were composed of thin lengths of wood, in the manner of Rietveld's furniture. The mirrors of the vanity became a playful part of the overall design, adding to it the shiny material, the unusual shapes, and the unorthodox and mobile supporting elements. The bed was a simpler design in which the different structural elements were distinctly

WOODEN FURNITURE (III)

The need for the Bauhaus to involve itself with industry was made plain by Gropius even before the exhibition. Some of the Bauhaus masters viewed such moves with resigned disapproval. For instance, the painter Lyonel Feininger wrote, with a certain foreboding, in October 1922:

Fig. 13. Room for a Woman, Haus-am-Horn, 1923. Breuer's vanity stool, known only in this photograph, had supporting elements extending straight down to the floor as legs.

...if we cannot show "results" to the outside world and win the "industrialists" to our side, then the prospects for the future existence of the Bauhaus are very dim indeed. We have to steer toward profitable undertakings, toward mass production! That goes decidedly against our grain and is a forestalling of a process of evolution?[21]

To some the shift in attitude from the earlier craft orientation of the school seemed sudden and extreme. But to those familiar with Gropius' writings of the prewar period, it was a return to the ideas which had been repudiated after the experience of the war. Since his appointment to the Bauhaus, Gropius had been well aware that the cooperation of the school with the local craft industry was considered essential for its survival. In 1923 he went a step further, attempting to bring the Bauhaus into

Fig. 14. Desk, gray maple, designed for the study niche in the living room of the Haus-am-Horn, 1923.

Fig. 15. Living-room cabinet built of gray maple, red paduk, Hungarian ash (all in matte finish), black polished pearwood, polished nickel fittings, and glass front, Haus-am-Horn, 1923. By 1923 most furniture made at the Bauhaus, including examples by Josef Albers, Erich Brendel, Alma Buscher, Erich Dieckmann, and Walter Gropius, reflected a variety of constructivist tendencies in European art.

an active cooperation with the mass-production techniques of modern industry. In the same year he wrote:

> It follows that the Bauhaus does not pretend to be a crafts school. Contact with industry is consciously sought...Craftsmanship and industry are today steadily approaching one another and are destined to merge into one...In this union the old craft workshops will develop into industrial laboratories: from the experimentation will evolve new standards for industrial production.[22]

Despite the Bauhaus' strong orientation toward craft, however, some designs were already suitable for mass production. The construction of Breuer's 1921 round table for the Sommerfeld house, for example, was uncomplicated, as were his 1923 designs for children's and adult side chairs (fig. 11) and, more important, his boxlike table (fig. 11). Although this rigidly geometrical table — its legs, square in section, running up into the top, without the visual break of a conventional overhang — was not executed until several years later, it was the earliest version of the now ubiquitous "Parsons" table. Variations of it were designed in the late 1920s by the German architect Mies van der Rohe and the French designer Jean-Michel Frank.[23] Breuer's widely published design, used extensively at the Bauhaus, was clearly their inspiration.

A slightly more complex table (fig. 16) was designed in 1924 and executed in cherry wood. Each of its legs, attached to the inside of the table frame, was placed at an angle perpendicular to the adjacent leg. It demonstrated a persistent constructivist impulse that can be seen even in Breuer's simplest furniture at this time.

Furniture designs by Breuer and other Bauhäusler using less expensive woods, especially plywood, and clearly intended for mass production, were more prevalent in 1924. Among these were Breuer's cabinets made for

kitchens or bedrooms (fig. 17). Characteristic of both were the use of brightly painted colors for decorative effect and a simplified construction that nonetheless permitted interesting designs.

More complicated than these was a combined desk and bookcase (figs. 18, 19), also made in painted plywood. Designed for use in the middle of a room or with one of its short sides against a wall, the desk-bookcase was still fraught with a de Stijl complexity of form and an emphasis on its "constructed" qualities. Again, Breuer used color to compensate for the loss of the texture and grain of fine woods.

One final piece of furniture that deserves mention in the context of Breuer's earlier wooden furniture is the chair (fig. 20) designed for, or at least used in, a housing development designed by Gropius and built in Dessau in 1926. Whether the chair already existed in 1924 or was a completely new design is not known. By 1926 Breuer was already designing furniture in tubular steel, but Gropius desired inexpensive mass-produced furniture for the houses, and wood was the logical answer. Breuer designed a side chair and stool for the project and may also have designed a

Fig. 16. Table, cherry wood, natural and dark stain, 1924.

dining table. The chair was similar to his earlier designs but different in the completely separate construction of seat and back units.

In 1924 Breuer completed his course of study and passed his journeyman's examination, becoming one of the few students who actually graduated from the Bauhaus. Armed with a letter of introduction to the editor of the avant-garde journal *Bulletin de L'Effort* *Moderne*, Léonce Rosenberg, he set off for Paris, where he had decided to pursue his career.[24] Rosenberg published two of Breuer's furniture designs in November of 1924 and introduced Breuer to members of the Parisian artistic community, including Fernand Léger. Shortly thereafter, Breuer found employment in Paris with an architect whose identity is unknown.

Fig. 17. Bedroom cabinet, plywood, 1924. Brightly painted in primary colors, the large cabinet was typical of many wall units designed by Breuer during this period.

Fig. 18. Two-sided desk-bookcase, plywood, 1924. Some of Breuer's designs were still fraught with a de Stijl–constructivist complexity of form.

Fig. 19. Bookcase side of double-sided desk-bookcase, 1924. The abstract design, which emphasized colored planes, was common to both furniture and architectural design of the period.

33

In September 1924, after Breuer had left the Bauhaus, the Thuringian government began a series of moves whose aim was to close the Bauhaus. Although the declared reasons were economic, it soon became evident that the motivation was essentially political. The city of Goethe and Schiller, of Nietzsche and Liszt, had decided that it had had enough of the strange artistic, social, and political activities of the Bauhaus. On 26 December 1924, the Masters of the Bauhaus declared the school dissolved as of 1 April 1925, the expiration date of their contracts. Negotiations were begun with other German cities to which the Bauhaus might possibly relocate, although its continued existence was not a certainty. Dessau, Frankfurt, Hagen, Mannheim, and Darmstadt were all considered as possible sites for the school. By March of 1925, it had been decided to move the Bauhaus to the city of Dessau. With the knowledge that the school would have a new home, Gropius wrote to Breuer in Paris and asked him to return to Germany to join the Bauhaus in Dessau as Master of the carpentry workshop. Breuer left Paris almost immediately.

Fig. 20. Walter Gropius, apartment interior at the Törten housing settlement, Dessau, 1926. Breuer designed the chairs, stool, and per- haps the table — pieces that Gropius requested for the entire housing development.

Bauhaus Dessau
1925–28

The city of Dessau is located on the banks of the Elbe River, a two-hour drive from Berlin The Mayor in 1925 was Dr. Fritz Hesse, a progressive interested in the arts and in modern industry. Through his efforts many new businesses, including the Junker airplane works, had come Dessau. The move to a city where planes were constantly flying overhead somehow seems appropriate for the orientation of the new Bauhaus.

Through Hesse's intervention, the city of Dessau allocated funds for the construction of a new complex of buildings for the school (fig. 22), including studios and classrooms, a dormitory building, and a group of four free-standing houses for the Masters.

All of the Masters with the exception of Gerhard Marcks, head of the ceramics workshop, and virtually all of the students moved to Dessau. The ceramics workshop was dropped and a new graphic-design section was added to the school. Along with Breuer, four other students were asked to join the new school as Masters: Josef Albers, Herbert Bayer, Hinnerk Scheper, and Joost Schmidt. Within a year's time Breuer would, according to Ise Gropius, become "the most important personality among the young masters."[25]

Although Gropius had, as early as 1922, renounced the primarily craft orientation of the school, the move allowed him to institutionalize further the declared changes in the

Fig. 21. The Bauhaus faculty, photographed atop the Bauhaus studio building, 1926. Left to right: Josef Albers, Hinnerk Scheper, Georg Muche, László Moholy-Nagy, Herbert Bayer, Joost Schmidt, Walter Gropius, Marcel Breuer (hatless), Wassily Kandinsky, Paul Klee, Lyonel Feininger, Gunta Stölzl, and Oskar Schlemmer.

Fig. 22. Walter Gropius, Bauhaus, Dessau, designed 1925, completed in 1926. The new Dessau Bauhaus buildings provided the suitably modernist setting for Breuer's first tubular-steel furniture designs.

Bauhaus philosophy. Marcks's decision not to travel to Dessau allowed the school to dissolve its most craft-oriented department. The various workshops were no longer led by a Master of Form; instead, each department had one Master who, beginning in 1926, was called Professor. Since the majority of the Masters were former students, it was felt that they were sufficiently grounded in their respective crafts to carry all of the teaching responsibilities.

During March of 1925, the Masters and many of the students arrived in Dessau. While Gropius worked on the designs for the new buildings, the Masters moved into temporary quarters in the Dessau Kunsthalle. It was during these months, probably between April and September, that Breuer designed his first tubular-steel chair.

FIRST TUBULAR-STEEL FURNITURE

The circumstances surrounding Marcel Breuer's development of modern tubular-steel furniture in 1925 long ago became a legend of the modern movement. The story, nonetheless, bears recounting.

Breuer's most exciting experience during his first weeks at the relocated Bauhaus had nothing to do with artistic matters, but centered around purchasing his first bicycle, an Adler, and learning to ride it. He was remembered by many as spending a great deal of time riding around the city. Breuer was impressed by his bicycle's strength and lightness, the result of its being made of tubular steel. This seemingly indestructible material could be bent into handlebar shapes and could easily support the weight of one or two riders; why then could it not be used for furniture?[26]

He went to the Adler company and attempted to interest them in the idea of tubular-steel furniture, but they showed no interest in the suggestion. He next went directly to the tubular-steel manufacturer, the Mannessmann Steel Works, inventors of the seamless extruded steel tube, and purchased for himself lengths of tubing bent to his specifications. He then hired a plumber (who better to work with the tube?), who helped him weld the steel tubes together.

It should be noted that in 1927 Breuer wrote: "I first experimented with duralumin, but because of its high price I went over to using precision steel tube."[27] But it is unclear whether Breuer experimented with aluminum before making his first chair or whether, in fact, the first models were made in aluminum. Part of the initial impetus to design in hollow metal was the extraordinarily light weight of the material, which greatly contrasted with Breuer's heavy wooden furniture. Aluminum was the lightest metal available, but it was extremely difficult to weld and was also far more expensive than tubular steel; it was therefore abandoned shortly after Breuer began working with metal.

During the spring and early summer of 1925, Breuer and his occasional assistants worked on the first experimental model of his tubular-steel furniture, a large club-type armchair (fig. 23). "In fact, I took the pipe dimensions [approximately twenty millimeters in diameter] from my bicycle. I didn't know where else to get it or how to figure it out," Breuer explained.

The first version of the armchair was a source of consternation for Breuer. The welding of the prebent pieces made the chair very stiff; it had no resilience, a quality he considered essential for comfort. The nickel-plate finish was found to be unsatisfactory and was also very expensive. Finally, the relatively lightweight but welded skeletal chair was bulky and difficult to store.

Without Breuer's knowledge, Lucia Moholy photographed the experimental version of the chair, and the picture was published in a local

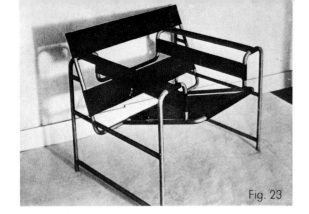

Fig. 23

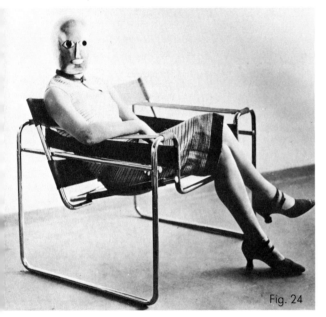

Fig. 24

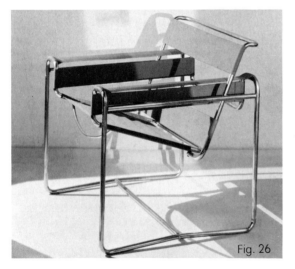

Fig. 26

newspaper while Breuer was still working on the design.[28] On the basis of the photograph he received many inquiries asking if the chair was available for purchase. He ignored the requests and continued working until he arrived at what he thought was the final solution for the design (fig. 24).

Breuer was extremely nervous about his new metal chair. In 1927 he wrote:

> Two years ago, when I saw the finished version of my first steel club armchair, I thought that this out of all my work would bring me the most criticism. It is my most extreme work both in its outward appearance and in the use of materials; it is the least artistic, the most logical, the least "cosy" and the most mechanical.[29]

Breuer's anxiety began to wane only after the chair was seen by Wassily Kandinsky, who praised it profusely. In January 1926 it was the centerpiece of an exhibition of Breuer's work held in the Dessau Kunsthalle.

Breuer's first tubular-steel armchair, which is now popularly known as the "Wassily" chair (for Kandinsky), a name it came to be marketed by around 1960, was essentially constructed of nine pieces of steel tubing, bent and bolted together, the nuts and screws visibly extending beyond the tubes.[30] After the first experiments, the chairs were constructed from steel bent in Breuer's own studio and were upholstered with a finely woven horsehair which is said to have had the appearance of a shiny, metallic canvas. The horsehair was far stronger than simple canvas, which was also used, and did not lose its shape. Once the chairs were put into large-scale production, a material marketed under the trade name of *Eisengarn*, or Ironcloth, was also used. *Eisengarn* was a canvaslike material formerly used only in military belts and boot laces.[31] It is unclear whether it was actually made from horsehair or was a reinforced canvas.

Fig. 23. Club armchair, tubular steel with fabric (possibly horsehair), 1925. Breuer's first tubular-steel chair was made from prebent lengths of tubing welded together; although braces joined front legs to back legs, the chair was still conceived of as having four separate legs.

Fig. 24. Club armchair, 1925. A Bauhaus student in a mask from Oskar Schlemmer's *Triadic Ballet* sitting in what Breuer considered to be his first "final" version of the armchair, which connected the legs of each side in a runner or sled arrangement, allowing for easy moving about; in addition to light weight and transparency, mobility was a characteristic sought by Breuer in his new furniture.

Fig. 25

Fig. 25. Club armchair, tubular steel and convas, late 1927 or early 1928. (Collection The Museum of Modern Art, gift of Herbert Bayer.) The definitive version of the armchair, in which Breuer connected the back uprights in a more continuous design.

Fig. 26. Club armchair, 1929. An alternative version produced by Thonet added a cross brace to the base and made the seat continuous with the outer frame, thereby altering the structure of the frame. Thinner braces were placed beneath the seat to supply lateral stability lost by the removal of the crosspiece that originally spanned the front of the seat.

The club armchair still partook of the de Stijl–constructivist aesthetic seen in Breuer's wooden chairs of 1922–23. All within the context of what is implied to be a cubic volume, the tautly stretched planes of fabric and the labyrinth of steel tubes turn the chair into an abstraction. The design makes the observer conscious, above all, of the interaction of planes in space. The polished metal framework forms an interlocking network of planes running parallel and perpendicular to each other. The upholstery, whether it be canvas, *eisengarn*, or leather, offers a highly successful contrast of texture, shape, and color with the frame. In many ways the chair seems deliberately and unnecessarily complex, even fussy; yet it possesses an integrity and a sense of artistic sophistication that have made it emblematic of the best avant-garde furniture of the 1920s.

Like Rietveld's Red-Blue chair (fig. 8) Breuer's armchair is a somewhat awkward design. The angling of the seat and back recalls the Rietveld design. A crucial difference, however, which becomes true of most of Breuer's seating furniture after 1925, is the sense the chair gives of the seat and back being suspended above the ground—or, more correctly, floating within a network of lines and planes. The sitter never touches the steel framework of the chair. The notion of suspending the sitter in pure space remained a constant one in his seating furniture, and should be recalled when the origins of the modern cantilever chair are discussed. Breuer's ideal of seating, as presented in the 1926 photomontage of a "Bauhaus film, five years long" (fig. 27), was the sitter floating on "resilient air columns."[32]

There was an unmistakable irony in Breuer's choice of the comfortable club armchair for his first tubular-steel chair. The furniture type was the subject of unrelenting vilification among many early modernist designers. No doubt the design of a chair with maximum support and the possibility of an intricate structure appealed to Breuer as a first project. Yet it was the one furniture type that seemed to defy the transparent and open aesthetic of the newly developing modern architecture, an aesthetic to which tubular-steel furniture was ideally suited.

In the 1927–28 version of the chair (fig. 25), the construction of the back from a single piece of tube was introduced to reduce the stress on the two separate back pieces found in the original design. Not only did it reduce the possible inward tilt of the pieces, but the joining of the back uprights led to a more homogeneous design, one with which Breuer was more satisfied. To a certain extent, however, the complicated constructivist aesthetic still remained in Breuer's first tubular-steel chair. Through the use of tubular steel a new beginning had been established, and would be built upon and clarified until the logic of the material could be fully expressed.

Breuer began producing a limited quantity of the club armchairs in late 1925 and sold them to those who had inquired when the photograph had been published. These chairs were made in his own studio, and the transactions were kept separate from the commercial ventures of the Bauhaus itself. Although there could have been no question that the artistic climate of the Bauhaus had everything to do with Breuer's ideas and designs, he has always spoken of his tubular-steel furniture as independent work. Asked if he considered the chair to be a Bauhaus product, he replied:

> The chair was not a Bauhaus product in the sense that a painting by Paul Klee was not a Bauhaus product. [Klee's painting] was done on his own time and with his own money, in his own workshop. To that extent it was not a Bauhaus product.

While Breuer produced a limited number of the armchairs, he also worked on new designs. In late 1925 and early 1926, he designed a set of folding theater chairs (fig. 29), a small stool (fig. 31), and a side chair (fig. 32). Although Breuer maintained that these designs were developed independently of the new Bauhaus buildings, he could not have been unaware that the radically new buildings called for new and appropriate furniture. According to Breuer, Gropius saw his new designs and asked him to produce large quantities of these three items of seating furniture for the new building. In addition, Breuer was asked to assist in the design of the interiors of the Masters' houses, on which construction had actually begun during the summer of 1925, before the main buildings were started.

By March of 1926, the exteriors of the school and Masters' buildings had been erected, and Breuer was at work on the interior designs. During the summer of 1926 the Masters' houses were completed; in September the studio wing of the main building was opened and in use. Finally, in October, the rest of the school buildings were unofficially occupied. The official celebratory opening of the school occurred on 24 December 1926.

FURNITURE IN THE SCHOOL BUILDINGS

The low, connecting section of the Bauhaus building, joining the studio and workshop wings, housed the auditorium and canteen, or dining room, on the ground level. The canteen had collapsible accordion walls at one end which opened to join it to the auditorium stage. Breuer furnished both of these rooms.

Breuer's tubular-steel theater chairs, first installed in and possibly designed for the Bauhaus auditorium (figs. 28, 29), were traditional tip-up theater chairs, similar in overall conception to Thonet's innovative bentwood theater seating of 1888. Much of the construction of the theater seats called for the welding together of parts. Only the armrests and seats were actually bent. The arms were welded to

1921

1921¹/₂

1924

1925

19??

Fig. 27. "Bauhaus film, five years long. Every day we are getting better. In the end we will sit on resilient air columns." As published in the *Bauhaus* magazine, July 1926.

the uprights of the frame, while the seat was bolted only to the front arm support on which it pivoted. A lateral rear support, which held the seat in its horizontal position, also served to attach and stabilize each seat to the adjacent ones. Both seat and horizontal bar were covered with small pieces of rubber at the contact points to prevent superficial damage and noise when the seats were raised or lowered. The seating was bolted to the floor at the base of each arm.

As in the design of the club armchair, the uprights of the back frame were not joined, but instead terminated at their highest point. The upholstery was sewn around each seat and also clamped to each of the back uprights. Like virtually all of Breuer's furniture, the theater chairs were carefully designed and meticulously detailed.

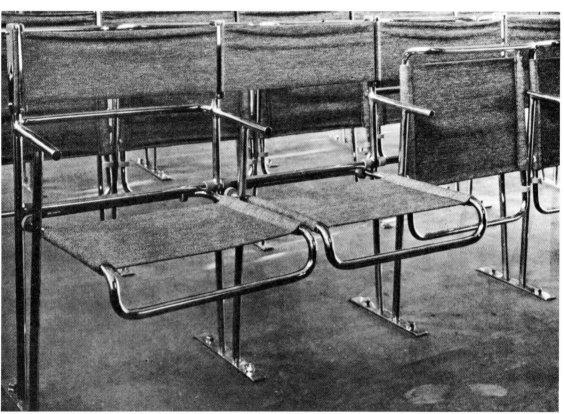

Fig. 28. Bauhaus auditorium, 1925–26. This was the first large-scale installation of tubular-steel furniture. The seating was by Breuer, lighting by the metal workshop under Moholy-Nagy's direction, and the color scheme by the wall-painting workshop under Hinnerk Scheper.

Fig. 29. Tubular-steel theater seating, 1925–26. Subsequently manufactured by Standard-Möbel and Thonet as model B1.

These seating units, through the use of the cantilevered seat, exploited the structural possibilities of tubular steel far more effectively than had the club armchair. The cantilevered arms, which recalled the wooden armchair of 1922, showed Breuer's predilection for arms which dispensed with visible supports.

For the adjacent Bauhaus canteen (fig. 30), Breuer designed, and the cabinetmaking workshop built, a series of long dining tables, extremely simple in construction and appearance, based on his design of 1923 (fig. 11). His new stool (fig. 31), another innovative design that brilliantly exploited the structural possibilities of tubular steel, was used for seating.

The stool, which was modified in size as a group of nesting tables in 1927, was a refined and elegant design — it was also Breuer's favorite. It was marked by a distinctive originality of conception that demonstrated Breuer's move away from the complications of constructivism toward a mode of design that was more personal. With the stool, he had designed what was arguably the simplest possible solution for a piece of tubular-steel furniture.

The shape of the stool was boxlike. Like other Breuer tubular-steel designs, it gave the impression of being a schematic diagram of a given furniture type. Made from two pieces of bent tubular steel, the stool was so successful because it was remarkably light, visually unobtrusive, the least expensive of all the tubular-steel designs, and could be used either as a stool or as a table. Testimony to its ingenuity was provided by both Mies van der Rohe and Le Corbusier, who designed stools which were clearly imitations of the Breuer original.

Breuer's stools were used throughout the school, in the studio building, and in the Masters' houses. Also used throughout the school, especially in office spaces and in virtually all of the Masters' houses, was Breuer's first tubular-steel side-chair design (fig. 32). Although used so extensively at the Bauhaus, this side-chair model was never produced commercially. In most versions of the chair the sections of steel that formed the back and rear legs flared outward both above and below the bottom of the back upholstery. This lent a certain awkwardness to the design. In addition, the joining of the two main units through the bolting together of two parallel horizontal lengths of round tubing, one atop the other, did not make for complete visual stability.

Problematic though some aspects of the design were, it did confirm Breuer's interest in working on chairs, and other furniture, that utilized a runner or sled arrangement for the base of the chair, rather than four separate legs. The importance of this element, first used by Breuer in the 1925 club armchair, cannot be overestimated. For although its origins may indeed go back to Thonet's bentwood rocking chairs, it was Breuer's tubular-steel designs that made the element an integral part of modern tubular-steel furniture. The initial impulse for the runners was to provide designs that were mobile not only because they were light in weight, but also because they could easily be pulled or pushed along the surface of the floor. This runner arrangement for chair bases became an important visual expression of the continuous nature of tubular steel, one of the most important structural (and intellectual) aspects of the new furniture. Part of the initial interest in tubular steel was the fact that it could, like certain woods, be bent. Steel, however, was easier to bend and offered potential that had so far barely been investigated. It must have seemed possible, at least on a theoretical level, for a chair to be made from a single, continuous, bent length of tube. The impulse toward designing chairs from a single piece of material has been a strong and persistent one in modern times. As technology improved and new materials and processes were invented, designers moved closer and closer to that goal. Tubular steel was the first

Fig. 30. Bauhaus canteen, 1925–26. The tables were designed by Breuer and built in the carpentry workshop, which Breuer now headed. The dark wall to the right folded to allow the extension of the auditorium stage into the canteen.

Fig. 31. Nesting stools, tubular steel and wood, 1925–26. (Collection The Museum of Modern Art, gift of Dr. Anny Baumann.) Each stool was made from two pieces of tube; the seats were attached with screws placed through the tube and the side of the seat; only in later years was the connection made with metal flanges. Both Standard-Möbel and Thonet manufactured the stool as a set of nesting tables, model B9.

material since the development of bentwood in the 1840s, to offer the opportunity for such furniture, even if it was necessary to add material—fabric, leather, caning—for seats and backs. The major problem, of course, was that a chair still needed four legs to stand on, even if the legs were joined to each other by continuous lengths of steel. And although Breuer's stool appeared to be a ''continuous'' design, the central design impulse of the period concerned the side chair or armchair. It was not until the development of the cantilevered chair in 1926–27 that the promise of a continuous chair became, at least in principle, fulfilled.

BAUHAUS MASTERS' HOUSES

The Masters' houses were a group of four Gropius-designed buildings located in a pine grove adjacent to the school. The Gropiuses lived in one entire house. The other houses were designed for two families each. The plans of the three two-family houses were nearly identical, with very large studio spaces a part of each. Unfortunately, only the Gropius and Moholy-Nagy quarters were extensively photographed, and those of Kandinsky and Georg Muche to a lesser extent.

For Wassily and Nina Kandinsky, Breuer designed a dining-room table and chairs in wood and tubular steel (fig. 33) and a set of bedroom furniture. The design of the dining-room set originated with Kandinsky's request to Breuer that he provide them with furniture based on the motif of the circle. The results pleased Kandinsky enormously, although Breuer regarded them as a rather frivolous formal exercise.

The chairs were composed of a boxlike base-seat unit with cylindrical legs, painted white at the top, joined together on three sides by rectangular pieces of wood and, in the front, by two lengths of tubular steel. The seat was an upholstered circle of wood trimmed in white. The backs were made from two tubular-steel supports and an upholstered wooden back, also rectangular.

Although the chairs suffered from a lack of harmony between the heavy base and the very thin and light back, the accompanying table was as beautiful a piece of sculpture as the contemporary constructions by the Hungarian artist and Bauhaus Master Moholy-Nagy, which it very much resembled. It was made from a rectangular wooden base (raised on four short lengths of tubular steel), from the top of which projected eight thin steel

Fig. 32. Side chair, tubular steel and fabric, 1925–26. Two main sections of tube, each made from several pieces, provided the frame of the chair, which was widely used at the Bauhaus but never put into mass production.

tubes supporting a circular wooden tabletop painted white. The tubes gave the top the appearance of floating in space. The whole formed a well-thought-out and harmonious composition. The table was so popular among the Masters that it was also made for the dining rooms of Gropius and Moholy-Nagy. The bedroom furniture, never photographed, consisted of beds, night tables, stools, and a dressing table built into the wall.[33]

All of the furniture designed for the Kandinskys, with the exception of its use of tubular steel, was similar in feeling to Breuer's earlier work. The request by Kandinsky that Breuer base the designs on the circular motif forced Breuer back into the more doctrinal approach typical of his earlier efforts.

Such was not the case with the built-in and free-standing cabinetwork that Breuer designed for the Gropius and Moholy-Nagy houses. Here was the first indication of Breuer's own enormous talent for designing what are now commonly referred to as wall units or wall

storage cabinets, but which were little used in 1925–26. Breuer has never been given sufficient credit for making these wall units an integral part of the interior architecture of the 1920s and '30s.

Gropius and Breuer collaborated on much of the Gropius house, Breuer designing all of the color schemes and all of the kitchen cabinetwork. And although the two men were jointly credited with the design of the wall units in most of the rooms, it seems likely that Breuer was chiefly responsible for these designs.

The built-in wall unit in the dining room (fig. 34) functioned as an oversize sideboard with storage spaces for all manner of tableware. Finished on both sides, it formed part of the wall between the pantry and dining room.

In the bedroom (fig. 35) and guest room the walls were likewise fitted with built-in cabinets, some flush with the walls, some projecting. In these rooms the breaking up of the wall surface with cabinets gave a remarkable degree

Fig. 33. Dining table and chairs, wood and tubular steel, the wooden parts painted black and white, 1925–26. Devised for the Master's house of the painter Wassily Kandinsky, the furniture fulfilled his request that the design be based on the motif of the circle.

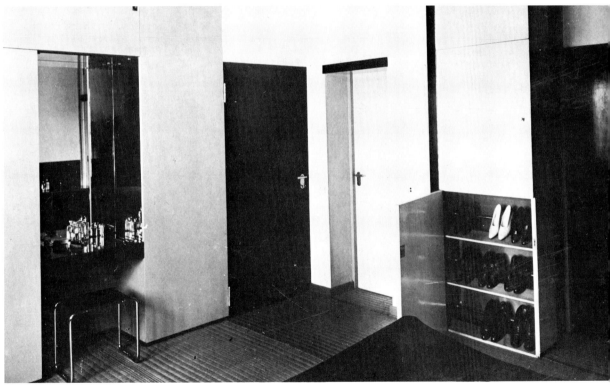

Fig. 34. Dining room, Gropius Master's house, 1925–26. The dining-room wall unit was one of many pieces of cabinetwork designed by Breuer and Gropius for the house. The wall unit had glass shelves above, cabinets with sliding doors on both the middle and lower levels, and one middle cabinet with fall front that formed a serving surface.

Fig. 35. Master bedroom, Gropius house, 1925–26. The sophisticated color scheme was designed by Breuer, while the interesting cabinetwork was credited as a collaboration between Gropius and Breuer.

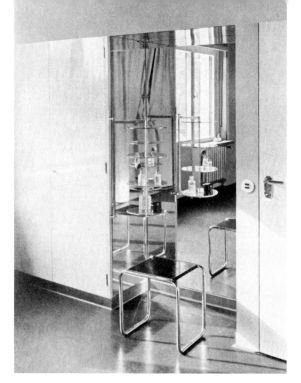

of animation. A cabinet for shoes and clothes projected, while the door to the bathroom receded into the actual wall space. And built into the bedroom and guest room were dressing niches surrounded on all sides and above by mirrors. In the guest room (fig. 36) Breuer built a tubular-steel pivoting glass-shelf arrangement, while in the bedroom (fig. 35) a vanity table was built into the space. On the floors of the rooms he used a form of oriental woven hemp matting that would become a hallmark of his interiors. (Although sometimes referred to as Japanese or Chinese matting, it was probably made in Indonesia and imported by the Dutch, who used similar floor coverings extensively.) In addition, in most of the rooms, thin painted borders marked baseboards and separated cabinet surfaces and doors from one another.

Fig. 36. Guest room dressing niche, Gropius house, 1925–26. Breuer designed the tubular-steel and glass multishelf dressing table.

Fig. 37. Double desk, Gropius house, 1925–26. The desk that Breuer designed for Walter and Ise Gropius was photographed at least a year after its completion with Standard-Möbel's B7 swivel side chair.

Besides his small stools, typical "Bauhaus" side chair, and Kandinsky dining table, all of which were used in the Gropius house, Breuer specially designed several new pieces of furniture. One was a long double desk (fig. 37), specifically requested so that Walter and Ise Gropius could work side by side. It was fitted with drawers, shelves, and storage space below the writing surface; above was a thin horizontal shelf unit. By their bedside, the Gropiuses had a pair of tables (fig. 38) made of wood, glass, and tubular steel. The combination of materials, in addition to the suspension of the glass shelf and the cantilever of the drawer, reflected the current interest at the Bauhaus in the combination of different materials in sculptural constructions.

One of the more innovative items of furniture in the house, credited as a collaboration between Gropius and Breuer, was a tubular-steel and wood-framed sofa (fig. 39), the back of which folded down to form a double bed. A cushion inserted with steel rods into the foot of the couch could be removed and placed at the head of the upper portion of the couch when it was unfolded to form a double bed.[34]

Moholy-Nagy's house contained many similar elements, also designed by Breuer, and a few more unusual ones. The living room (fig. 40) was furnished not only with Breuer's tubular-steel furniture, but also with a pair of wooden couches set against the walls, a rectangular wood coffee table with dark glass top, and an unusual bookshelf-storage unit projecting into the middle of the room. Undoubtedly painted in many colors, it served to block off the dining room from the living room and to help define the furniture grouping against the wall. One of the surfaces of the storage cubes included a sliding extension for a typewriter; the stool served as the typing chair.

In the Moholy-Nagy dining room (fig. 41) was a wall unit similar in overall conception, if

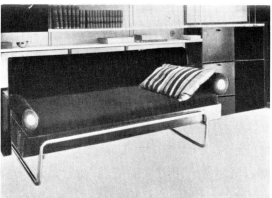

Fig. 38. Bedside table, Gropius house, 1925–26.

Fig. 39. Gropius and Breuer, "Double sofa," living room, Gropius house, 1925–26. The back of the couch dropped down to form one half of the bed; the round cushion that was inserted with steel rods at the foot of the single bed could be moved to become the headrest for the top of the double bed.

49

Fig. 40. Dining room, Moholy-Nagy house, 1925–26. Furniture designed by Breuer, color scheme and easel painting by Moholy-Nagy, and lighting fixture by Gropius and the Bauhaus metal workshop.

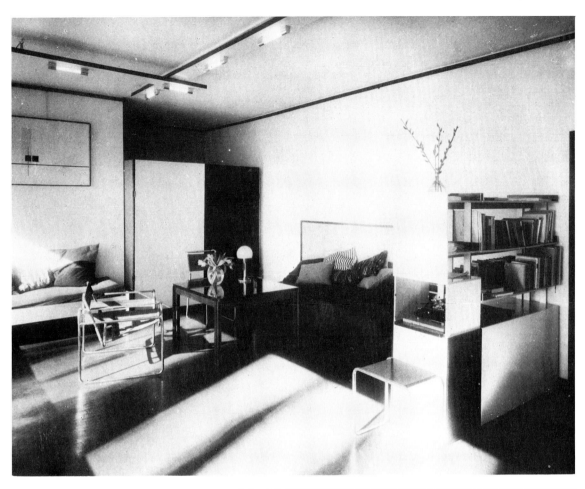

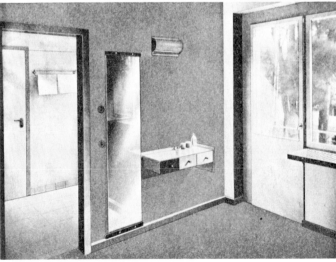

Fig. 41. Living room, Moholy-Nagy Master's house, 1925–26. Breuer designed most of the furniture in the room, including the ingenious projecting wall-storage unit.

Fig. 42. Bedroom-bath, Moholy-Nagy house, 1925–26. The use (and asymmetrical arrangement) of the dressing table and mirror became standard in Breuer interiors.

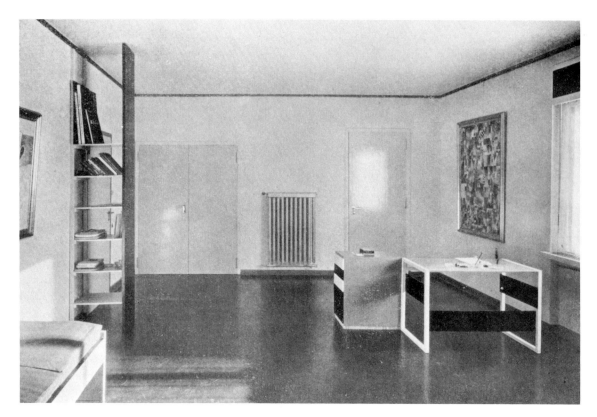

not of identical design, to the Gropius unit. It too opened both on the pantry and dining sides. The bedroom contained a dressing mirror and table arrangement (fig. 42) which Breuer had used for Nina Kandinsky and which he would employ over several decades.

The extent of Breuer's involvement in the interior design of Georg Muche's austere interior (fig. 43) is unclear. He designed an unusual desk and drawer unit, and possibly another group of modular drawers, which sat in the middle of the Muche living room. The desk was a simple boxlike construction placed perpendicular to a drawer unit. Like much of the Masters' house furniture, the desk and drawer were painted in black, white, and bright colors such as blue or red. Breuer may also have designed a couch and thin bookcase that projected from the living-room wall.

TUBULAR-STEEL FURNITURE AND STANDARD-MÖBEL

On 12 September 1926, after the Masters' houses had been finished and as the students were moving into their new facilities, Breuer applied for a design registration (*Gebrauchsmuster*) for seven furniture designs:[35] the stool, the club armchair, a folding club armchair, the side chair, a version of the same chair with arms, the theater seating, and a drawing-table frame made from tubular-steel sawhorses (fig. 44). Neither the armchair version of the Bauhaus side chair nor the drafting table is to be found in photographs of the Bauhaus interiors, although the drafting table was published a few years later.

Shortly after Breuer's application for the registration of his designs, he became involved with a company that sought to market his

Fig. 43. Living room, Georg Muche Master's house, 1925–26. The desk and drawer unit were part of a series of modular designs which Breuer worked on in 1926.

tubular-steel chairs. The firm, Standard-Möbel, later known as Standard-Möbel G.m.b.H. and then as Standard-Möbel Lengyel & Co., was begun by another Hungarian architect, Kalman Lengyel, in partnership with Breuer. Although the founding date of the company is unknown, Lengyel must have come to Breuer either in late 1926 or early 1927 and proposed a joint business venture. As Breuer later recalled, Lengyel offered to supply all of the money and staff necessary to start a company that would manufacture and sell Breuer's furniture to the public. The ensuing business transactions were never handled through the official Bauhaus corporation or through its business manager, but rather, directly between Breuer and Lengyel. In view of Gropius' desire not only to have Bauhaus goods produced under license, but also to publicize designs that were in any way related to the school, the

independent relationship that Breuer always maintained with producers of his early furniture, designed at the Bauhaus, is difficult to explain. Yet the explanation lies simply in Breuer's insistence that the designs were his own independent creations and had nothing to do with the school itself. Although Ise Gropius noted in her diary that "In spite of his youth, he [Breuer] is really the only one who understands what it means to run this Bauhaus,"[36] the reaction to Breuer's announcement of his new business venture was one of dismay.

A very unpleasant event with Breuer. He has made a deal about his metal chairs with a Berlin friend without telling anybody and that will now lead to great difficulties in the negotiations of Dr. König in Dresden about a Bauhaus GmbH [a limited corporation established in 1926 to license the manufacture

Fig. 44. Tubular-steel frame for drafting table, 1926. A pair of tubular-steel sawhorses joined by two lengths of tubing in a continuous design formed each side of the frame; the table was never mass-produced.

of Bauhaus products and insure income for the school]. Dr. König is quite upset about the fact that just now during the final negotiations one of the most important pieces of the enterprise has been removed, and he has written a very outspoken letter to Breuer about this.[37]

Indeed, some of Breuer's fellow teachers felt that he lacked sufficient interest in the welfare of the Bauhaus community as a whole and was far too concerned with himself.

The earliest record of Standard-Möbel's existence is the exhibition of their furniture at a housing exhibition in June 1927. Around that time they probably issued their first catalog (fig. 45), which was designed by Breuer's Bauhaus friend and colleague Herbert Bayer and printed by the Bauhaus printing press. This catalog featured eight designs, all by Breuer and all listed with model numbers beginning with the letter B.[38] The designs already seen at the Bauhaus were: B1, the fabric-covered unit of theater seating, also available with wooden seat and back as B2; B3, the club armchair; and B9, the stool. There were four new models. B4, the folding armchair (fig. 46), designed in 1926, was advertised as especially appropriate for "boats, playing fields, terraces, summer houses, gardens, and garden cafés." In many ways a folding chair best symbolized the new furniture, being the most mobile, the easiest to

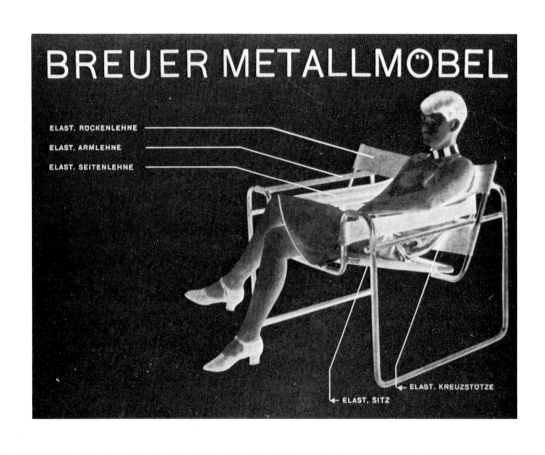

Fig. 45. Herbert Bayer, cover of catalog designed for Standard-Möbel, printed by the Bauhaus printing press, probably 1927. (Collection The Museum of Modern Art, Tschichold Collection, gift of Philip Johnson.) Standard-Möbel was the company started by Kalman Lengyel with Breuer in late 1926 or early 1927 to market Breuer's tubular-steel furniture designs.

Fig. 46. Folding club armchair B4, tubular steel and fabric, 1926. Manufactured by Standard-Möbel and exhibited in one of the Gropius houses at the 1927 Weissenhof exhibition.

Fig. 46

Fig. 47

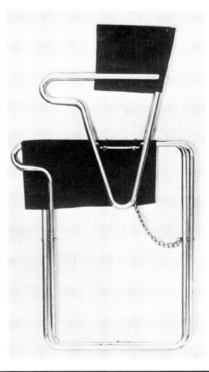

Fig. 48

Fig. 47. Folding side chair B8, tubular steel with wood seat and back, 1927. Although this chair was never illustrated in Standard-Möbel catalogs and its model number was later given to several stool designs, it was described in a catalog of 1928.

Fig. 48. Folding armchair, tubular steel and fabric, c. 1928. The design demonstrated Breuer's fascination with folding chairs, but apparently it was never mass-produced.

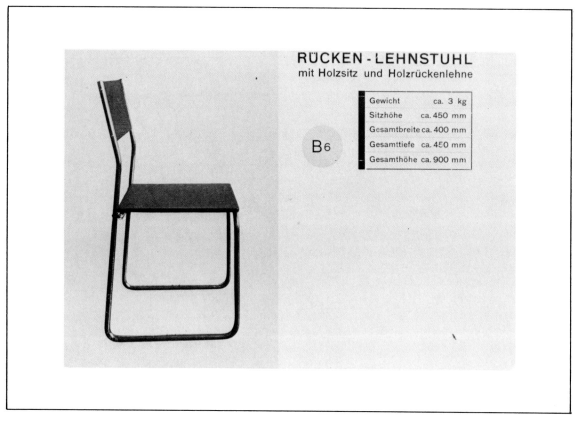

RÜCKEN - LEHNSTUHL
mit Holzsitz und Holzrückenlehne

B 6

Gewicht	ca. 3 kg
Sitzhöhe	ca. 450 mm
Gesamtbreite	ca. 400 mm
Gesamttiefe	ca. 450 mm
Gesamthöhe	ca. 900 mm

store, and the most adaptable of all chairs. Breuer designed a simpler folding side chair in 1927 (fig. 47), the wooden seat of which folded straight up into the frame. In the following year he designed a more complex "director's" chair (fig. 48) with canvas seat and back. Neither chair was ever produced in quantity. Even the B4 was not a commercial success. It remained in production for no more than three years.

B6 (fig. 49) was a modest side chair which could be seen as a variation of the B9 stool. The basic form of the stool was retained for the seat and a wooden back was added. It was the least costly of the side chairs and was probably intended for institutional use. B7, the swivel desk chair (fig. 37), which the catalog suggested was appropriate for use not only in offices but also in kitchens, consisted of a simple L-shaped seat and back, the back tilted slightly to the rear and raised on a well-proportioned four-legged base. The height of the seat was adjustable.

The B5 side chair (fig. 58) can be seen as a successful refinement or further development of the Bauhaus side chair (fig. 32). Indeed the overall conception of the design was the same; only the construction of the front legs differed substantially.

Most of the chairs above, included in the first Standard-Möbel catalog, were designed in late 1926 or early 1927. A second Standard-Möbel catalog was printed in mid-1928. It was a large foldout brochure entitled "Das Neue Möbel" (the new furniture), featuring the "Breuer tubular-steel furniture system." In addition to four new Breuer designs of 1927, four furniture items marked with the letter *L*

Fig. 49. Side chair B6, tubular steel and wood, 1926–27. From the Standard-Möbel catalog designed by Herbert Bayer (see fig. 45).

(for Kalman Lengyel) were also offered.

Variations of existing Breuer designs were seen in the B11 armchair (fig. 50), an arm version of the B5 side chair, and in the B12 table, which was the B9 stool with a shelf added. Included in the price list but not illustrated was a stool with the same measurements as the B9, but with a soft fabric top. The completely new designs were a large bed, B13, and the more interesting table, model B10 (fig. 51).

The B10 table, which became one of the most widely plagiarized tubular-steel designs of the 1920s and '30s, demonstrated Breuer's fascination with the ideal "continuous" tubular-steel design. The table was not, of course made from a single length of tube, but from several. In order to give the illusion of an uninterrupted line, however, Breuer connected the bottoms of each pair of corner legs with small U-shaped pieces of tube. Although fault may have been found in the proportions of the table—the parallel lengths of steel at the legs made it seem a bit squat—the overall design was ingenious. It was exactly this type of design that opponents of tubular steel loved to ridicule (fig. 63).

INTERIORS, 1926-28

While Breuer taught at the Bauhaus, he received a number of commissions for interior designs, most of them through Gropius. Breuer's large-scale architectural work existed only in project form; and in view of the economic climate in Germany at the time, and in view of his youth, he was fortunate to be able to design a number of apartment and house renovations and several exhibition interiors. Gropius' high regard for Breuer's work was manifested when he published the twenty-three-year-old Breuer's project for a large apartment building in his important 1925

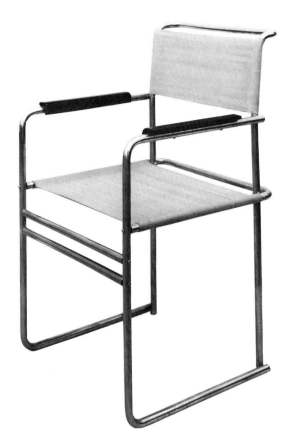

Fig. 50. Armchair B11, tubular steel and convas, 1926–27. (Collection Manfred Ludewig, Berlin.) The simplified geometric design of the B5 side chair and B11 armchair made them the most popular tubular-steel chairs of the 1920s; it was not until 1930 that cantilevered chairs became widely available and popular.

Fig. 51. Table B10, tubular steel and wood, 1927. (Collection The Museum of Modern Art, Estée and Joseph Lauder Design Fund.) Breuer's table was one of the most widely plagiarized designs of the period; imitations were manufactured by companies on the Continent, in England, and in America.

Fig. 52.. Thost house, Hamburg, 1926. Part of an entire-house renovation, this neo–de Stijl room was designed to house the clients' pottery collection.

Fig. 53. Thost house, Hamburg, 1926.

survey of European architecture, *Internationale Architektur*, which featured the work of all of the major progressive architects of the early twentieth century; the second edition of the book (1927) contained two Breuer projects. And as much as Breuer's projects could be seen in the context of the New Architecture developing in Germany, Holland, and France, his executed interior designs shared the new modernist spirit with the interiors of many avant-garde European architects. These new modernist interiors, like much of the architecture of the period, boldly proclaimed their objectivity, their complete rejection of the past, and their appropriateness to a new, modern way of life. They developed during the 1920s and spread through the exchange of ideas between designers, through the publication of projects and completed work in magazines and books, as well as through exhibitions which played a pivotal role in spreading the new gospel.

Among the earliest commissions of which photographs survive was the Thost house in Hamburg of 1926. The clients, a wealthy young couple, had a large pottery collection, which the illustrated room (figs. 52, 53) was designed to house. Although Breuer's vocabulary was predominantly de Stijl, the elements were handled with grace and intelligence by the twenty-four-year-old designer. Built into or projecting from the walls were a large couch, a table, and a series of vitrines for the display of pottery. The wood, glass, and metal projecting vitrines were more unusual than the orthodox de Stijl table made from a large lacquered top placed upon an asymmetrical T-shaped base. The base of the table was attached to the projecting base of the adjacent vitrine, which in turn ran into the base of the built-in couch. A simple lighting fixture hung from the ceiling, and the floor was covered with oriental matting. The combining of the different materials, finishes, and textures became an important element of Breuer's work at this time. The only known photographs of the room were taken before the installation of the Thosts' pottery collection or any pictures which might have hung on the wall. These, of course, would have imparted a warmth to the room and helped relieve the stark austerity seen in the photographs. But even with them the room's overall modernity must have been quite shocking.

Breuer's use of built-in or free-standing cabinet units of varying shapes and sizes became one of the most common features of his interiors. One handsome free-standing cabinet (fig. 54), intended for use against a wall, was designed in 1926 for an apartment in Berlin. It was more complex in design than Breuer's typical modular units, although the wide variety of colors and materials were all confined within a regularized rectangular shape. A remarkable degree of transparency and of sculptural effect was achieved not only through the use of glass or open surfaces on the front, but also through the insertion of glass panels on one side of the cabinet and at the top of each side, which broke up the essentially boxlike form. The contrast of the basically symmetrical design of the piece with controlled attempts at asymmetry in the handling of the different parts of the unit greatly enhanced the design.

More characteristic of Breuer's interiors was his use of smaller cabinets (fig. 55) placed against, or more often hung from, the wall. Around 1926 Breuer designed a system based on a module of thirty-three centimeters, a system he used in virtually all of his commissions from 1927 on. The most typical units were sixty-six centimeters in height and depth and were hung directly from the wall, although occasionally they were also supported by tubular-steel legs extended from the floor. In whatever combination of shapes and sizes, they added a regularity of shape and dimen-

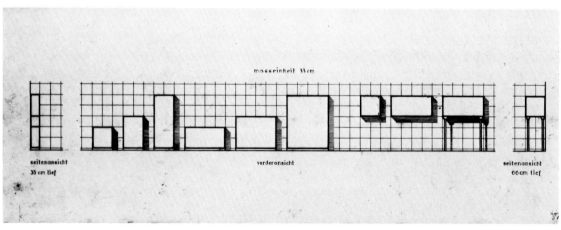

Fig. 54. Wall cabinet, wood, glass, and metal, designed for the Wilensky apartment, Berlin, 1926. The back panels were painted white (upper left), deep blue (upper right), and red (lower right); the fronts were either black lacquer or glass; the cabinet frame was made in a richly veneered plywood.

Fig. 55. Design for modular wall units, c. 1926. Based on a module of thirty-three centimeters, such cabinets were used by Breuer in virtually all of his interiors.

sion to his interiors, and stood in contrast to his earlier, more complicated constructivist forms. The beauty of the modular system was that the units could easily be executed by any carpenter from the drawings and could be made less or more expensive through the use of different woods, different types of fronts (sliding or pivoting, wood or glass), and different finishes or trims (stain or lacquer, no trim or metal-plated edges).

In 1927, Breuer was commissioned to renovate the apartment of one of the best-known members of the European avant-garde, the theater producer Erwin Piscator. With his left-wing politics Piscator resembled numerous Bauhäusler, and his role in the development of modern theater was seminal. He had had much contact with Gropius and Moholy-Nagy, and in 1927 Gropius designed a project for a Total Theater for Piscator, a daring architectural experiment that would, through a mobile design, allow different types of performances to be staged in the same hall.

Unfortunately, as is the case for virtually all of Breuer's commissions, no plans or drawings survive; according to Breuer, they were all removed from the attic of his Berlin apartment building and destroyed during the early 1930s. But, like many of the Berlin dwellings that Breuer subsequently renovated, the Piscator apartment was a large, sprawling space in an old building. It contained at least six rooms of large size (figs. 56-59). Perhaps the most dramatic space was the dining room (fig. 56). As in most of Breuer's newly renovated apartments, he stripped the walls of moldings, leaving them completely bare and, in all likelihood, painted white. Here, as in all of the rooms, he painted the baseboard a dark color. The long dining room was fitted with a thin, horizontal band of hanging storage units, on top of which selected objects were placed for decorative effect. The dining table was formed from a wooden top (covered with milky glass)

that sat on two bases painted in a dark color. Each base looked like an expressionistically rendered letter *H* placed on its side, and the table, with its dramatic silhouette, provided the only angular shapes in the entire room of verticals and horizontals.[39] Piscator's dining room was a carefully balanced composition, spare and severe, yet with a unique sense of drama achieved through the meticulous placement of the various objects in the room.

The bedroom of Mr. Piscator (fig. 59) (as usual, there were separate bedrooms for married couples) could more properly be termed a bedroom-gymnasium. Typical of the period, and especially of modern architects, was the concern with health and physical fitness—what Breuer termed the "healthy body culture." Virtually all early modern architects designed their houses with wide expanses of windows to allow maximum exposure to daylight, terraces for sunbathing, and some even with gymnasiums. Large-scale, low-cost housing schemes were designed with maximum attention to hygiene. To many there existed a direct correlation between good health and modern architecture, as there was between poor health and traditional buildings. Tubular steel was, in particular, praised by its proponents for its hygienic qualities.

The obsession with health resulted in international hygiene exhibitions and the heroic depiction of athletes in the work of such avant-garde artists as Willi Baumeister, El Lissitzky, and John Heartfield. And although this interest in health could be seen in the context of the rise of Hitler and the glorification of the Aryan race, such concerns were typical of architects of all nationalities. In 1923 the French architect Robert Mallet-Stevens designed a sports terrace adjacent to an indoor swimming pool for a villa in Hyères, and at the 1925 Paris Exposition des Arts Décoratifs, the French designer Francis Jourdain had exhibited a "Salle de Sport." In the section on

"The Manual of the Dwelling," in his 1923 *Towards an Architecture*, Le Corbusier wrote:

> Demand a bathroom looking south... opening if possible on to a balcony for sun baths; the most up-to-date fittings with a shower-bath and gymnastic appliances....
> Never undress in your bedroom. It is not a clean thing to do and makes the room horribly untidy....
> Demand a vacuum cleaner....
> Demand ventilating panes to the windows in every room.
> Teach your children that a house is only habitable when it is full of light and air, and when the floors and walls are clear.
> To keep your floors in order eliminate heavy furniture and thick carpets...[40]

The furnishing of Piscator's bedroom was austere. The bed was enclosed in a half-canopy arrangement attached to a small wardrobe. The cabinets were probably painted in gray-blue and contrasting white, a color scheme typical of those years. The wall surrounding the bed was covered with fabric, a common means to protect the wall finish. (Breuer is said to have favored a light, woven, strawlike material commonly available under the name "madagascar.") An entire wall was devoted to carefully arranged exercise equipment, which was used by Piscator each day upon rising.

In June of 1927, the enormously important Deutscher Werkbund exhibition, "Die Wohnung" (The Dwelling), opened on the grounds

Fig. 56. Dining room, Piscator apartment, Berlin, 1927. Three spherical light fixtures were hung from the ceiling, adding to the abstract geometry of the room.

Fig. 57. Living room, Piscator apartment, Berlin, 1927. Sliding doors separated the dining and living rooms; placed above the radiator were cacti, often called *the* plant of the modernist interior.

Fig. 58. Living room, Piscator apartment, Berlin, 1927. The room was furnished with tubular-steel furniture including an unusual coffee table made of glass and tubular and sheet steel; above the couches was a unique track-lighting system constructed from a long length of tubular steel to which was attached a simple bulb reflector.

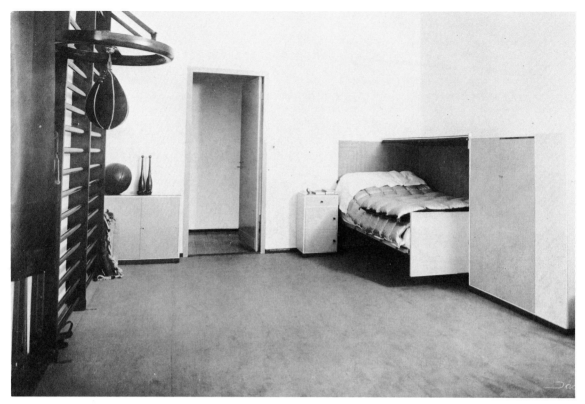

of the Weissenhof estate in Stuttgart. The Weissenhof exhibition, which included thirty-three housing units designed by sixteen leading modernist architects, not only was the first and most important of the housing exhibitions of the 1920s, but marked the first time that the architectural work of the major figures of the newly developing modern movement could be seen at one time in one location. Although Breuer was not among the group of architects invited to design the housing units, he did, thanks to Gropius' recommendation, design rooms in the houses designed by Mart Stam and Gropius.[41] In addition, his furniture was exhibited in a coordinated exhibition in the Stuttgart Gewerbehalle organized by Lilly Reich.

·According to Breuer, Stam officially hired him to execute the rooms in his houses, and in 1926 sent Breuer the plans of the new designs so Breuer could work on the interiors. In one of the Stam houses, Breuer designed a study and a dining room (fig. 60). The study was a stark room fitted with a single-board desk hung from a wall and attached to a group of modular bookshelves, drawer, and cabinet units, all executed in sheet metal. Breuer considered the design of the units conventional and the use of metal unnecessary since the cabinets and shelves could easily have been made from wood.[42]

The dining room was equally spare. The same modular bookcases and cabinets were used in a different arrangement, stacked against one wall. The glass-topped table and metal furniture was by now familiar. The floor was linoleum, a popular flooring material during the 1920s and '30s because of its shiny appearance and ease of maintenance. More often, however, it was used in exhibition interiors,

Fig. 59. Bedroom, Piscator apartment, Berlin, 1927. Typical of the 1920s obsession with health and physical fitness was the extensive use of gymnasium equipment in Mr. Piscator's bedroom. By 1927, having such equipment in one's home was quite fashionable—even among those who probably never made use of it.

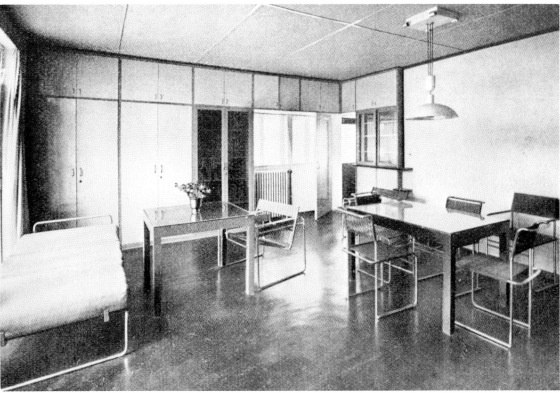

Fig. 60. Dining room, Mart Stam house, Weissenhof housing exhibition, Stuttgart, 1927. In the Stam house Breuer made use of modular enameled metal cabinets of his own design. His interiors at this time relied increasingly on metal furniture, glass-topped wooden tables, and linoleum floors.

Fig. 61. Dining-living room for Walter Gropius house, Weissenhof housing exhibition, Stuttgart, 1927. The far wall was entirely covered with built-in cabinet units; the daybed to the left may have been specially designed by Breuer; the lighting fixture was manufactured by the firm of August Blodner.

which received heavy wear, rather than in houses, where a warmer and softer-textured material was desired for bedroom, dining room, or living room.

The extent of Breuer's collaboration with Gropius on the interiors of his houses is unclear. The relationship between the two was so informal that Gropius may have purchased the furniture without consulting Breuer. Nevertheless, Gropius credited Breuer with the design of a dining room for one house and a dining-living room (fig. 61) for another. In their furnishings both rooms were similar to the Stam dining room; the larger dining-living room had an entire wall of built-in cabinet and storage spaces.

The Weissenhof exhibition marked the coming of age of the first generation of tubular-steel furniture. Through the publication of photographs of Breuer's first tubular-steel designs and of the Bauhaus interiors, and through the visits of numerous architects to the Bauhaus, the news of Breuer's tubular-steel furniture had spread throughout the progressive European architectural community. When the Weissenhof exhibition opened in June 1927, not only were most of the designs produced by Standard-Möbel exhibited, but also new tubular-steel furniture designs by leading architects, including Mart Stam, Mies van der Rohe, J. J. P. Oud, S. van Ravesteyn, Heinz and Bodo Rasch, and Arthur Korn. Until that point most metal furniture was made by the architects themselves or by manufacturers producing in very limited quantities. The Weissenhof exhibition evoked wide discussion of tubular steel and sparked the interest of larger companies in its manufacture.

TUBULAR STEEL AND THE NEW INTERIOR

All of Breuer's tubular-steel furniture was characterized by simplicity of design and construction, physical and visual lightness and transparency — the most sought-after attributes of the new, mass-produced furniture. A Standard-Möbel advertisement of 1928 proclaimed:

> tubular-steel furniture with fabric seat, back and armrests is as *comfortable* as well-upholstered furniture, without having its weight, price, unwieldiness and unsanitary quality. one type has been worked out for each of the required kinds of uses and improved to the point where no other variation was possible....due to its durability and sanitary quality Breuer metal furniture is approximately 200 percent more economical in use than ordinary chairs.[43]

The marketing lines were clearly drawn: tubular-steel furniture should be purchased because of its strict rationalism ("one type for each use...improved to the point where no other variation is possible") and its superiority over ordinary chairs, especially the overstuffed armchair. The language of the advertisement was typical of the message and tone adopted by advocates of tubular-steel furniture.

The emphasis was somewhat different in a statement on "metallmöbel und moderne raumlichkeit," written by Breuer:

> metal furniture is part of a modern room. it is "styleless," for it is not expected to express any particular styling beyond its purpose and the construction necessary thereof. the new living space should not be a self-portrait of the architect, nor should it immediately convey the individual personality of its occupant.[44]

The architect's objectivity, the removal of his presence and that of his client from the design, was viewed as an important step toward establishing the supposedly timeless, styleless spirit of the new architecture and design. The spirit of modern times, wrote Breuer, must be reflected in the places we inhabit:

> since the outside world today subjects us to the most intense and diverse impressions,

we change our ways of life in faster sequence than in former times. it is only natural that our environment will also be subject to corresponding changes. this brings us to furnishings, spaces, buildings, which are alterable, mobile, and variously combinable in as many of their parts as possible.

Flexibility and mobility lead to transparency, openness, freedom, and spatial dynamism:

> the furniture, even the walls of the room, is no longer massive, monumental, apparently rooted to the ground or actually built-in. instead, it is broken up airily, sketched into the room, as it were; it impedes neither movement nor the view through the room. the room is no longer a composition, nor a rounded-off whole, since its dimensions and elements are subject to substantial alteration.

The inherent rationality of the overall conception of the room is reinforced by the fact that metal is the appropriate material for furniture. It is, as usual, contrasted to the heavy, upholstered armchair:

> i purposely chose metal for this furniture in order to achieve the characteristics of modern space elements just described. the heavy, imposing stuffing of a comfortable chair has been replaced by a tightly fitted fabric and some light, springy pipe brackets. the steel [parts] used…are remarkably light, though they withstand severe static strain… the sleigh shape increases flexibility, all types are constructed from the same, standardized elementary parts, which may be taken apart or exchanged at any time.
>
> metal furniture is intended to be nothing but a necessary apparatus for contemporary life.

Steel becomes the only appropriate material: light, resilient, elementary, standardized, and interchangeable. Metal furniture not only becomes desirable or appropriate, but the dogmaticism of the modern movement takes over and metal furniture becomes "a necessary apparatus for contemporary life."

Like other early modernist designers, Breuer believed in a mode of design that was impersonal, purely functional, and made up almost exclusively of straight lines (which were described by Georg Muche as "the formal idiom of the modern architect"[45] and by Le Corbusier as "the grand acquisition of modern architecture").[46] The appearance of the new design would not, according to Breuer, be dictated by "the everlasting and arbitrary changes of form, color, and style," but rather, strictly by the functional requirements of the object and the necessities of modern machine production.[47] In Le Corbusier's famous words, "We must look upon the house as a machine for living."[48]

Tubular steel became the necessary and appropriate furniture for the new modernist interior and for the modern way of life. Until 1925 Thonet bentwood had been the mass-produced furniture most in favor with progressive architects. Bentwood furniture was light, visually transparent, appeared to derive its form from the manufacturing process, and was completely modern in appearance. Tubular steel, however, achieved all those characteristics but was devoid of reference to the past—as bentwood was not—and partook of the mechanistic imagery that captured the spirit of the period.

Breuer and many of his colleagues were imbued with the spirit of *Amerikanismus*. He had read the best-selling autobiography of Henry Ford, and saw in his assembly-line production of cars the potential for manufacturing all the component parts of modern architecture and design. In furniture, as in all aspects of design, Breuer and his contemporaries sought forms and materials that not only showed the impact of large-scale factory production, but also symbolized it. This machine-oriented aesthetic was perceived as a widely shared and modern one that in its ideal form relied on the collective input of designers all moved by the same spirit.

and couches appeared which were strictly metallic in character, and were efficient and about as interesting as modern sanitary fittings.[49]

He associated metal-furniture designers with what he called "robot modernism."

> The metal furniture of the robot modernist school can claim fitness for purpose, and it exemplifies a just and original use of the material. It expresses the harsh limitations of the movement to which it belongs, even as Le Corbusier, who might almost be regarded as the voice of the movement, expresses with lucidity and relentless logic its utter inhumanity.

Gloag, along with many others, was particularly upset by the use of metal furniture in the domestic interior:

> Although metal equipment may be satisfying to the standards of commercial life, and may adequately resist the wear and tear of an office, there does not appear to be any case for substituting metal for wood in furniture that is designed to give convenience and harmony to the home...
> The designer may devise an interior in which chairs of shining aluminium are an essential part of the composition; but in such schemes human beings appear intrusive; there is no sympathy between them and the setting.
> Metal is cold and brutally hard and...gives no comfort to the eye.

Other writers, such as the French designer and writer Maurice Dufrêne, who wholeheartedly delighted in the decorative schemes of what is now termed Art Deco, found the uniformity of the new furniture to be its most depressing quality:

> The same chair, mechanical and tubular, is to be found in almost every country.... It is the anonymous, neutral, universal chair...
> And this is the root of Dullness....
> The machine has beauty, but this beauty

Breuer was well aware of what he described as the "severe rationalism" of his new designs. Recently he stated that with his invention of modern tubular-steel furniture he had become "afraid of the criticism of others, afraid of my own criticism. I thought they would talk me out of it." Today the ubiquity of the tubular-steel chair makes that sense of the extremity and novelty of the new furniture difficult to imagine (figs. 62, 63). Yet there were designers, critics, and consumers who were not so convinced of the "necessity" for tubular-steel furniture, and who vehemently opposed its use. The English writer John Gloag was a knowledgeable observer of furniture design, but was also outraged by the widespread use of metal furniture. He sardonically noted that Germany

> ...began to lead Europe in the expression of mechanical art. Dramatic possibilities of design in metal were discovered...and chairs

Fig. 62. Karl Rössing, "The Young Aesthete," woodcut, 1929. The effete dandy of the 1920s declared his modernity by sitting in Breuer's club armchair.

68

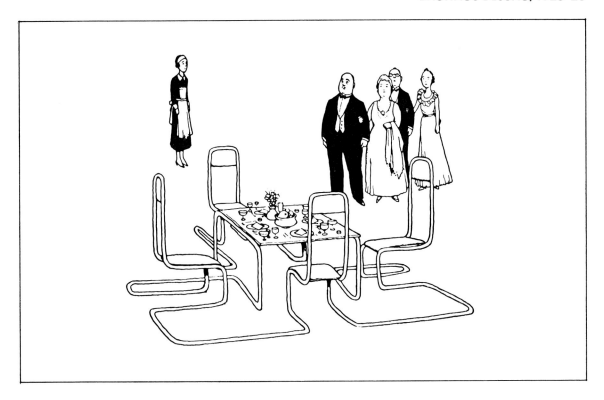

only exists in the movement which animates it, in the practical force which it generates. The beauty of the machine is not actually present. It is a potential beauty…But to demand of the machine…the same emotions as are aroused by a work of art which comes from the soul and heart…is nonsensical…

To construct a bed according to the same aesthetic as a suspension bridge, or to construct a house like a factory, to design a dining room as a chilly laboratory, shows a lack of psychology.[50]

Comparisons of tubular-steel furniture with the equipment of hospitals and doctors' offices were common. In 1930, five years after Breuer had made his first tubular-steel chair, and by which time he had virtually ceased to design in metal, no less a writer than Aldous Huxley wrote disparagingly of metal furniture, including Breuer's, exhibited at the 1930 Paris exhibition:

[Metal furniture] will be modern with a vengeance. Personally I very much dislike the aseptic, hospital style of furnishing. To dine off an operating table, to loll in a dentist's chair—this is not my idea of domestic bliss…the time, I am sure, is not far off when we shall go for our furniture to the nearest Ford or Morris agent.[51]

The proponents of tubular steel, of course, were not swayed from their belief in the material. As early as 1927, Breuer had addressed these attitudes when he wrote:

Our work is unrelenting and unretrospective; it despises tradition and established custom. A frequent criticism of steel furniture is that it is cold, clinical and reminiscent of an operating theater. But these are concepts which flourish from one day to the next. They are the product of habit, soon destroyed by another habit.[52]

Fig. 63. A satirical English view of tubular-steel furniture was provided in Robinson and Browne's *How to Live in a Flat* (1936), which explained to its readers that "Whereas formerly the best furniture was made by carpenters, cabinet-makers, and similar skilled craftsmen…nowadays the trade is almost entirely in the hands of plumbers, riveters, blow-pipers, and metal-workers of all sorts."

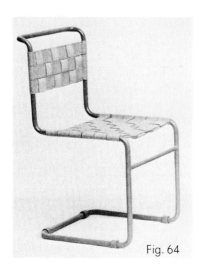

Fig. 64

Fig. 65

Fig. 66

THE TUBULAR-STEEL CANTILEVERED CHAIR

Perhaps the most revolutionary of the new tubular-steel designs was the cantilevered chair, the chair with two legs, which was exhibited and sold for the first time in 1927. Although Breuer has sometimes been credited with designing the first cantilevered chair, there is no doubt that the Dutch architect Mart Stam was the first to make a tubular-steel chair of cantilevered construction. At a meeting on 22 November 1926, held in preparation for the Weissenhof exhibition, Stam sketched the new chair he was working on, which was constructed from pipes and somewhat clumsy standard pipe fittings.[53] Among those present at the meeting was Mies van der Rohe, who, inspired by the drawing, also began working on a cantilevered chair. The chair that Stam showed at the exhibition (fig. 64) was made by the firm of L. & C. Arnold and was constructed from bent steel tubing painted black, with a seat made from canvas strips, and small round pieces of rubber attached to the base. Stam also exhibited a cantilevered lounge chair with arms (fig. 65) of similar construction, but with a leather seat and back. Several weeks after the Stam chairs arrived at the Weissenhof exhibition, Mies unveiled his new designs for a tubular-steel side chair and armchair (fig. 66). Aside from their great elegance and sophistication, Mies's chairs surpassed Stam's in being far more springy and resilient.

According to Breuer, a further chapter should be added to the history of the cantilevered chair. By his account, he had been working on the idea of a cantilevered chair during 1926 and continued to construct his chair because he was unable to work with tubular steel of proper diameter. All of his early furniture had been made from Mannessmann tube steel approximately twenty millimeters in diameter. Breuer calculated that he would need tubing of twenty-five millimeters in order to support the weight of a person in a chair that had only two legs.

Breuer has stated that he had begun research into the possibility of making a cantilevered chair after his first tubular steel designs were produced. The design of his B9 stool, when turned on its side, provided the stimulus for the idea. In that position the stool could be seen as the base, legs, and seat of a cantilevered chair; all that was necessary to complete the transformation was the addition

Fig. 64. Mart Stam, side chair, tubular steel and canvas, manufactured by L. & C. Arnold, 1927. Stam designed the first cantilevered tubular-steel chair in late 1926 or early 1927 from pipes and pipe fittings; for the Weissenhof exhibition he made this version in rigid steel tubing.

Fig. 65. Mart Stam, lounge chair, tubular steel and leather, 1927. A lesser-known Stam cantilevered chair, also exhibited at Weissenhof.

of a back. Further, Breuer has maintained that Stam visited the Bauhaus during 1926 and that the two designers spent time together both in Breuer's studio and on a journey by train to Frankfurt. At that time Breuer showed Stam all of his tubular-steel furniture and explained his idea for the cantilevered chair. Stam, Breuer recalled, mentioned nothing about any of his own experiments with tubular steel.

Although Breuer's account does put the Stam design in a different perspective, there is no definite record that Stam visited the Bauhaus in 1926. It *is* known that in 1926 Gropius attempted, unsuccessfully, to convince Stam to join the Bauhaus faculty. A trip to the school may therefore have taken place. Further, it is also known that Stam traveled in Germany during 1926, but his only certain destination was Frankfurt.

Although some may insist that owing to Breuer's development of modern tubular-steel furniture, the idea of cantilevered seating was in the air, and that the question of who made the first design should not be an important concern, it is nonetheless of considerable interest. It is not beyond reason that Breuer had conceived of a cantilevered chair based on the B9 stool or even on his simple B5 side chair (since with its rear legs removed, the B5 side chair closely resembles the Stam chair). And the idea of cantilevered seating was, at least in abstract terms, suggested in Breuer's 1926 "Bauhaus film, five years long" (fig. 27), where a woman reclines on "resilient air columns." But the abstract idea or description gives no suggestion of form. It was the Stam chair that provided the formal basis, throughout Europe, for the many cantilevered chairs that followed.

BREUER'S FIRST CANTILEVERED DESIGNS

In 1927, or perhaps as late as early 1928, Breuer designed his first cantilevered side chair, which was marketed by Thonet in early 1929 as model B33 (figs. 67, 68). By 1928 Breuer had also designed at least one arm-chair model, later marketed as B34 (figs. 69, 70), and a different cantilevered design that would become his most famous chair, the Thonet model B32 (fig. 71), along with an armchair version, B64 (fig. 72).

The B33 side chair, which can be seen either as deriving logically from Breuer's earlier work or as modifying slightly the Stam chair, was design reduced to the barest minimum. The chair appeared to be made of a continuous length of tube with the seat and back stretched between the sides of the frame. Its proportions and overall detailing were superior to those of the Stam side chair. There were no extra supporting members visible, no four legs to hold the chair up. And it is not difficult to believe that people were afraid to sit in the first cantilevered chairs.

The B34, of which there were two versions (figs. 69, 70), attempted to take the form of the simple cantilevered chair and turn it into an armchair. In both versions the most important modification to the side-chair design was the construction of the chair from two basic units: the L-shaped seat and back set within the base-leg unit (which itself took the form of the B9 stool tipped on its side).

In his masterful B32 chair (fig. 71) the continuity of the steel frame was broken. Because of the strength of the wooden seat and back frames, no additional support was necessary: no crosspieces, no hidden tubes beneath the seat, not even the usual joining of tube behind the sitter's back. A new dimension was added in this chair through the textural and coloristic contrast of the highly polished steel tubing with the wooden frames and the caned seat and back. The caning made the seat and back transparent and was also an unmistakable reference to the bentwood and cane chairs of Thonet, which had enjoyed a tremendous re-

Fig. 66. Ludwig Mies van der Rohe, side chair, tubular steel and leather, 1927. (Collection The Museum of Modern Art, gift of Edgar J. Kaufmann, Jr.) Based on a drawing of the Stam chair, Mies's chair was a more refined and sophisticated design, made from good-quality, highly resilient tubular steel.

vival of popularity during the mid-1920s. There was an added visual richness obtained through the manner in which the seat and back seemed to ride parallel to the planes of the tube, while remaining just barely separate. This was quite different from the B33, where, as in most of Breuer's chairs, the canvas wrapped itself around the tube, visibly attached to it. We are aware that the seat and back of the B32 are attached to the tube of the chair, yet visually, especially in profile, there is no indication of a bond.

The armchair version of the B32, model B64 (fig. 72), was structurally quite different from earlier Breuer armchairs. The design of the frame, especially that of the arms and back, was quite daring. The base and seat frame were similar to those of the side chair, with the exception that the tubing to which the seat was attached slanted in toward the center of the seat. From the back of the seat two parallel lengths of tube rose behind the back, just high enough to support it firmly, and then reached their way around both sides of the back to form the arms. The treatment of the arms as separate and hovering was dynamic and effective.

It is important to note that virtually any of the tubular-steel chairs produced in a given year will differ in detail and in dimension and proportion from those manufactured in another year. This is especially the case with the B32 and B64 models. The explanation for this lay in the increasing refinement of the methods for manufacturing both tubular steel and tubular-steel furniture. The years between 1925 and 1935 saw the birth and maturation of the new tubular-steel furniture industry. As more furniture was produced, and more manufacturers entered the field and increased competition, new methods were developed for manufacturing both the material and the furniture itself. For example, with the improvement of steel technology the strength of steel tubes was increased, and gradually tubular steel could be made both stronger and thinner. As a given chair was produced, and tested through years of use, new methods of con-

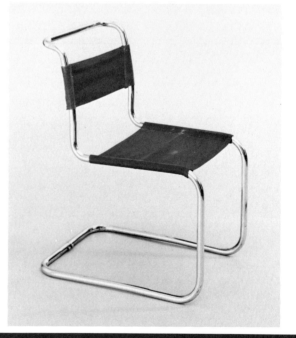

Fig. 67. Thonet side chair B33, tubular steel and canvas, late 1927 or early 1928. Ruled by the German courts to be an imitation of the Stam cantilevered side chair, it was credited to Stam beginning in 1932. Thonet first produced the B33 in late 1928 or early 1929 as Breuer's design.

Fig. 68. Thonet side chair B33½, tubular steel and canvas, 1929. (Collection The Museum of Modern Art, gift of Dr. Anny Baumann.) Child's version of Thonet's B33.

struction or modifications in design were introduced to make a less-expensive and sometimes better product. Most of the tubular-steel designers, including Breuer, felt that these modifications were improvements. Anything that would lead to the simplification of the production process, lowering costs to producer and consumer, was considered a distinct advantage.

ANTON LORENZ AND THE BUSINESS OF TUBULAR STEEL

By the time Breuer had designed his first cantilevered chair, and by which time Standard-Möbel had issued at least one catalog, a man named Anton Lorenz had become involved with Standard. Lorenz has for long been an obscure figure who was known to have purchased the rights to, and possibly even designed, tubular-steel furniture.[54] From 1928 on, during the 1930s and '40s, Lorenz was the plaintiff in lawsuits against virtually all of the large manufacturers of tubular-steel furniture; he charged them with plagiarizing his furniture designs. He is the key to explaining why the origins of the early cantilevered chairs became so confused.

Lorenz was born in Budapest in 1891. He taught history and geography there until 1919, when he moved to Leipzig with his wife, an opera singer who had been offered a contract to sing there. In 1920 he went into the lock business and became successful enough to move to Berlin, where in 1927 he met Kalman Lengyel, who had already founded Standard-Möbel, and who was looking for a firm to make the small line of Breuer's furniture in larger quantities. At the beginning of 1928 Lorenz came to an agreement whereby he began to manufacture the chairs in his own metal workshop, and became general manager of Standard. Breuer had little contact with his partners and concentrated on his own design work.

In mid-1928 Lorenz, and possibly Lengyel, persuaded Breuer to sign over to Standard-

Arch. Marcel Breuer

Fig. 69. Thonet armchair B34 (first version), tubular steel and canvas, 1928. Both Breuer and Anton Lorenz claimed the design. Lorenz' own company, DESTA, began manufacturing the chair only at the end of 1929, months after Thonet began production. The treatment of the cross brace spanning the legs is quite uncharacteristic of Breuer.

Fig. 70. Thonet armchair B34 (second version), tubular steel and canvas, 1929. Breuer modified the armchair design and arrived at a more successful solution for bracing the seat to the frame. Thonet also manufactured Breuer armchair B30, which differed only in its having the L-shaped seat and back directly welded to the arms and legs.

Fig. 71. Thonet side chair B32, tubular steel, wood, and cane, 1928. (Collection The Museum of Modern Art, Edgar J. Kaufmann, Jr., Fund.) Breuer's most famous and now ubiquitous seating design was attributed to Mart Stam on the grounds that Stam owned an artistic copyright on the principle of the straight-legged cantilever in chairs. Breuer was unquestionably the designer, and even after the court decision Thonet continued to pay him royalties on the chair.

Möbel the rights to his designs already in production. He did so to help save the company, which was doing poorly because of Lengyel's early mismanagement. He did not, however, sign over the rights to many new designs on which he was working. Because of its precarious financial condition, Standard-Möbel elected to produce only a limited number of items, and Breuer's new designs were not even considered for production.

At the same time, Breuer began negotiating with Gebrüder Thonet, most likely with Wilhelm Eitner, the director of their German branch, for an arrangement that would give Thonet the right to produce Breuer's new tubular-steel designs. An agreement was reached in July of 1928. Possibly at the end of 1928, but certainly by January of 1929, Thonet was advertising Breuer designs and, in a new advertising practice, crediting the individual designer for his work. Probably in January, but certainly by July, Thonet was selling Breuer cantilevered

chairs. The first Thonet catalog of tubular-steel furniture was devoted exclusively to Breuer designs and was issued during 1929.

Several surprising facts emerge from a close scrutiny of the chronology of these events. In November of 1928 Standard-Möbel was still advertising Breuer's club armchair and the "System Marcel Breuer." The coffee table (B18) advertised by Thonet in January of 1929 was not a model produced by Standard-Möbel. It is therefore clear that both Standard and Thonet were producing different Breuer designs during late 1928 and the first quarter of 1929. It was not until 11 April 1929 that Thonet puchased Standard-Möbel from Lorenz, including the rights to all of the other Breuer designs. In a gesture of good faith by Thonet, and in a desire to keep its most prolific designer of tubular-steel furniture, Thonet signed a new contract with Breuer for all of his designs.

In early 1929 Lorenz was engaged in a series of activities that would cast doubts on aspects of his sale of Standard to Thonet, create confusion as to who had actually designed the cantilevered chairs that Thonet was producing under its agreement with Breuer, and, shortly thereafter, plunge all of the parties into a massive lawsuit that would drag on for years.

After joining Standard-Möbel in 1928, Lorenz decided that the chair with the greatest possibility for commercial success was the cantilevered chair designed by Mies (fig. 66). Mies, however, rebuffed Lorenz' offers of a business partnership. Lorenz therefore approached Stam, designer of the first, if less interesting, cantilevered chair (fig. 64). Stam, who was about to leave Germany for Russia, agreed to discuss a business proposition with Lorenz. At the same time, Lorenz registered, on 12 February 1929, an armchair version of Stam's cantilevered side chair, which he claimed to have designed during 1928. This design, however, may already have been in production by

Fig. 72. Thonet armchair B64, tubular steel, wood, and cane, 1928. (Collection The Museum of Modern Art, purchase.) Following the court decision, Breuer's armchair design was also reattributed to Anton Lorenz, who as owner of Stam's original artistic copyright, as well **as his own design registration for a cantilevered armchair, held a virtual monopoly on cantilevered chair designs. Both B32 and B64 chairs were marketed as the "Cesca" chair (named for Breuer's daughter) only beginning in 1960.**

Thonet under Breuer's name; Thonet now had a contractual arrangement with Breuer.

On 18 June 1929, Lorenz and Stam came to an agreement whereby Lorenz assumed all rights to the Stam cantilevered side chair. Between July and September of 1929, Lorenz sued Thonet, claiming that the firm was producing two cantilevered chair designs that were protected by an artistic copyright (the Stam chair) or a design registration (the Lorenz arm version) in his (Lorenz') name. Finally, in September of 1929, Lorenz began a new tubular-steel company, Deutsche Stahlmöbel, or DESTA, which issued its first catalog in October. The catalog offered both the B33 and B34 models, as ST12 and SS32. The B33 and B34 models were sold in Thonet catalogs beginning in 1929 and attributed to "Arch. Marcel Breuer."

Lorenz' suit was against Thonet; Breuer was not directly involved as a defendant, only as a witness. The suit charged that Thonet was producing designs that belonged to Lorenz and for which Thonet had never secured the rights.

Thonet's case as put forth before the court stated that (a) the Stam chair (fig. 64) was not an original invention, that it was based on earlier Breuer designs, especially the B5 side chair (fig. 57), and that Stam should never have been granted a copyright for a design which was not original. Walter Gropius, among others, testified on Thonet's behalf that the Stam chair represented the logical development of Breuer's B5 and that it was an imitation of Breuer's design. Anticipating the plaintiff's response, Thonet continued that (b) even if the artistic copyright had been properly granted, the Stam chair was substantially different from model B33 (fig. 57) designed by Breuer. The B33 could not therefore be an infringement of the Stam copyright. Finally, (c) no matter what the copyright situation, Thonet argued it had legally purchased both designs

from the plaintiff in April 1929, along with all of the assets of Standard-Möbel, which included all the other Breuer Standard-Möbel designs. Among the contents of the Standard-Möbel workshop were four prototype models for B33 and B34 that had been made by Standard-Möbel employees, on company time, and with company equipment and supplies. Even if Lorenz claimed to have had a hand in their design, he was, at the time, an employee of the company. Therefore the designs were now owned by Thonet.

The County, Supreme, and Appeals Courts all ruled in Lorenz' favor. The Appeal decision stated that (a) there was no proof that Stam's chair was an imitation of any previous Breuer model, including the B5 side chair, and that at most the Stam chair represented "free use of the Breuer model."[55] Therefore, Stam had legally been able to secure an artistic copyright on his rectilinear, tubular-steel cantilevered chair. The court continued that (b) although it was true that the Stam chair was made of "lacquered, cast (non-resilient) steel tubing," and that the Breuer-Thonet model B33 was made from "nickel-plated precision steel tubing," the Breuer chair was so similar to the legally registered Stam design that "model B33 cannot be recognized as an original design...but simply as an imitation of the Stam chair." Finally, (c) Lorenz' registration of the cantilevered side and armchairs was in his own name, not in the name of Standard-Möbel. He was not required to turn over his personal property when he sold Standard-Möbel to Thonet. Lorenz had, the court noted, even offered to pay Thonet for the time and material involved in the manufacture of the four prototype chairs.

The result of these decisions was that Lorenz, who now owned the original Stam design, was confirmed as the sole owner of an artistic copyright on the aesthetic or artistic principle of the straight-legged cantilever in side chairs and armchairs. Thonet was forced to make a settlement with Lorenz based on previous sales, and, if Thonet wanted to continue manufacturing straight-legged cantilevered chairs, the firm would have to recognize the patents and registrations owned by Lorenz. The trial (at least this aspect of it) finally ended in 1932, after which all Thonet catalogs carried new designer credits for cantilevered chairs.[56] All side chairs were attributed to Stam, all armchairs to Lorenz. This applied even to the B32, B46, B55, and B64, on which Thonet continued to pay royalties to Breuer. Breuer was denied his royalties on B30, B33, and B34, and, according to his own account, became so exasperated that he ceased to design tubular-steel furniture.

Many facts were not, of course, revealed in the court decisions. Concerning the viewpoints of the various parties involved, it is known that Breuer regarded Lorenz as a "patent brigand." Lorenz, he felt, had plagiarized his designs, taken advantage of him, and carefully orchestrated the entire scenario. Gropius, among others, supported Breuer in this view. Thonet officials felt that Lorenz had misled or cheated them by withholding certain designs from them when he sold Standard. Further, they believed that he had cunningly manipulated the patents and registrations so that he could convince the court that the designs he owned held precedent over the earlier Breuer designs.

Lorenz, on the other hand, felt that he was the victim of a gross patent infringement by Thonet, and of a swindle by Breuer. Lorenz saw himself as a businessman with technical training who had the ability and knowledge to help designers exploit their talent and realize the full potential of their designs. Architects and designers, Lorenz felt, lacked the acumen necessary for good business. He believed in taking every advantage provided by the law to increase business.[57] In Lorenz'

mind, Eitner (of Thonet) and Breuer had allied themselves in a conspiracy to pirate the Stam and Lorenz designs. In what Lorenz termed the "Breuer swindle," Breuer had executed the original working drawings for the Stam chairs, and then taken the drawings to Thonet, claiming them as his own.

The ultimate irony of all this was that Lorenz' hand was so strengthened that he spent the next decade suing or threatening suit against virtually every manufacturer of straight-legged cantilevered chairs of any material and description; he became so mired in court cases that finding time for other work became difficult. After Breuer designed his vastly different aluminum furniture for the Embru company in 1932, Lorenz forced him, under threat of suit, to form a brief-lived partnership. (It was dissolved in 1936.) Under a similar threat, Mies van der Rohe was forced into a partnership with Lorenz in 1934 that covered all of his cantilevered designs. Despite this, when Lorenz found himself stranded in the United States at the beginning of the war in 1939—during a visit to a licensee, the Heywood-Wakefield Company, to discuss pending lawsuits against infringers of Lorenz' American patents—Mies felt sympathetic enough toward him to extend financial assistance.

Even Alvar Aalto was subject to Lorenz' threats. In 1937 Lorenz warned Artek, the Finnish manufacturers of Aalto furniture, that they had violated many of his (Lorenz') patents for cantilevered furniture. Lorenz had finally taken notice of Artek when their annual sales began to increase substantially, at the same time that he was planning to market cantilevered wood chairs designed by Mies. With the outbreak of the war, Lorenz was forced to abandon his attempts to sue Artek.

Lorenz' own company, DESTA, which produced designs by Stam, Erich Mendelsohn, Hans and Wassili Luckhardt, and others, was liquidated in 1933, at which time Lorenz sold the designs, but not the company, to Thonet and began to devote his energy to the research and development of reclining chairs. He invested all of the money he had been awarded in the Thonet lawsuit, contracted with a well-known scientific institute to carry out extensive research on body dimensions and mechanics, and with the architect Hans Luckhardt eventually patented mechanisms and designs for adjustable reclining chairs with tubular-steel frames. After Lorenz immigrated to the United States, he contracted with the Barcolo Company to market a new, upholstered version of his adjustable reclining chair as the Barca Lounger, one of the most popular chairs of the postwar period, one which appeared to be completely unrelated to the progressive designs Lorenz had previously marketed. In 1964 Lorenz died.

TABLE DESIGNS, 1928

While this myriad of business maneuvers proceeded during 1927 and 1928, Breuer continued to design tubular-steel furniture, none of which was produced by Standard-Möbel. The designs show the considerable range of

Fig. 73. Thonet table B19, tubular steel and glass, 1928. (Collection The Brooklyn Museum, gift of Mr. and Mrs. Alexis Zalstem-Salessky.) For his tables, Breuer adapted gummed rubber connectors used in plumbing to attach the steel and glass without the use of bolts or screws.

Fig. 74. Table designs B18 (top left), B27 (top right), B26 (center left), B23 (center right), typing table B21 (bottom left), and étagère B22 (bottom right), 1928.

Fig. 75. Thonet lounge chair B25, tubular steel and rattan, 1928–29. (Collection Manfred Ludewig, Berlin.) First sold by Thonet in 1929, Breuer's design made inventive use of coiled springs to suspend the seat from the rigid frame.

Breuer's talents and his prototypical tubular-steel solutions for different types of furniture. Most of the designs were first produced by Thonet at the end of 1928 or in 1929. They were first offered to the public in a small fold-out brochure, dating from after April 1929, which closely followed the format of the earlier Standard-Möbel brochure. It contained most of the designs previously sold by Standard-Möbel, with the exception of the B1 theater seating, the B4 folding armchair, the B11 armchair, and the B13 bed. All of the earlier designs offered were identical with the Standard-Möbel models. Ten new designs were offered.

Tables B18 (fig. 74) and B19 (fig. 73) were among Breuer's most accomplished designs. Both tables had rectangles of tubular steel placed within the frame. The boldness of this member was intended for effect rather than function, although with heavy glass and the uses required of a table, some type of extra bracing was necessary. The use of thick glass tops above the frames echoed the added rectangle of tubular steel and created the illusion of forms floating in a studied sculptural construction. Each of the elements was articulated as a separate entity, interacting with the other forms. The combination of the two materials was enormously successful, the insubstantiality of the glass serving to emphasize the steel structure.

A slightly different effect was achieved in the B27 table (fig. 74), the first Breuer design to make use of a more unusual and complex frame consisting of two identical, essentially V-shaped or open triangular units that upon first glance appear to have been made from two large, open rectangles, arranged in a cross shape. These elements abut each other but remain independent, at least to the eye; in fact, they were screwed together at both contact points and, in some examples, were welded together on the underside of the base.

Related to the B27 was folding table B26

B 46
Thonet

Fig. 76. Thonet armchair B46, tubular steel and canvas, 1928–29.

Fig. 77. Thonet armchair B55, tubular steel and canvas, 1928–29. (Collection Manfred Ludewig, Berlin.) Neither the B46 nor the similar B55 was a particularly popular chair during the 1930s, despite the originality of the designs.

(fig. 74), a design which was only briefly in mass production. The idea behind it was simple enough: two rectangles of tubular steel, the base of one shaped to pivot on the other. Once closed, the tabletop folded, allowing easy storage. Problems with the design were said to have caused this table, along with all of Breuer's folding chairs, to be dropped from the product line.

Also offered in the first Thonet steel catalog were three less significant designs that were variations on the B9 stool. Models B21, B22, and B23 (fig. 74) all demonstrated the extent to which Breuer was able to adapt similar designs to a number of different needs and forms. When, in 1930, Thonet began producing a larger number of designs, the company went even further in exploiting Breuer's designs as well as transferring details.

FURNITURE DESIGNS, 1928–29

The last group of Breuer's tubular-steel furniture, designed for the most part in 1929, were included in Thonet's largest tubular-steel catalog the following year. The catalog illustrated approximately thirty models attributed to Breuer. In some cases Breuer was credited for designs that were not his (see Appendix 1); in others he was not credited with furniture he is known to have designed. Among those models adapted from designs that had never been previously mass-produced were table B14 (figs. 84, 87), armchair B30, and bed B701.

The B25 lounge chair (fig. 75) was made from a frame based on the B9 stool, with a free-floating seat and back suspended from the frame by a pair of coiled springs that were

Fig. 78. Thonet lounge chair B35, tubular steel and canvas, 1928–29. (Collection The Museum of Modern Art, Estée and Joseph Lauder Design Fund.) Breuer's armchair varied in structural detail from year to year and was available with a wide variety of upholsteries. The conception was of a chair made from a continuous length of steel.

the most unorthodox part of the design. They made the chair look like the "machine for sitting" to which many modernist designers aspired. The back was adjustable and could be raised or lowered through the use of a support which fitted into the arms of the chair. Although the springs stretched under the weight of the sitter, they were strong enough so that the overall lines of the chair were not seriously deformed when it was in use. Yet the effect for the sitter could be almost that of a rocking chair where only the suspended seat and back moved within the rigid frame. The seat and back were in woven rattan which, in most circumstances, would have been covered by upholstered cushions. Unfortunately this resulted in a somewhat clumsy appearance, depending on the considerable bulk of the cushions.

Armchairs B46 and B55 (figs. 76, 77) represented a more fanciful chair design, quite uncharacteristic of Breuer's work. There is no doubt, however, that he was the designer. The central feature of both chairs was an unusual arm that emphatically curved behind the seat, adding a strong curvilinear element to an essentially rectilinear design. In both chairs, the backs were formed from a completely separate length of tube, while the base, front legs, seat, and arms were all articulated as a single piece.

Among the more complex and successful of Breuer's cantilevered chair designs was the B35 lounge chair (fig. 78). Breuer's idea for a cantilevered lounge chair was vastly different from most contemporary designs, where the original side chair or armchair merely had its proportions changed so that it could serve as a lounge chair. With possible references to the club armchair of 1925, Breuer fitted the B35's cantilevered seat into what might be seen as a rectangular volume. The structural frame of the chair served to outline diagrammatically the rectangular box, and the long seat floated

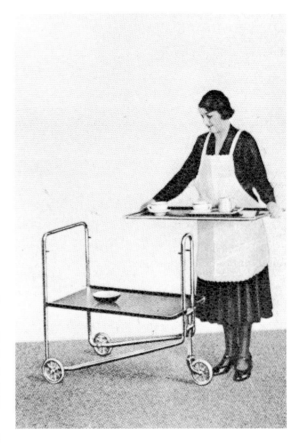

freely between the arms as a true cantilevered design. More unusual was the sense that the chair was formed from a continuous length of tube, beginning with one arm and winding its way along the outline of the chair to the end of the other arm.[58]

The final new design was B54 (figs. 79, 99), a three-wheeled tea cart which Breuer was to use in many of his interiors. The top shelf of the cart was removable for use as a serving tray. With its spoked wheels and pronounced hardware, it partook of the mechanistic imagery that most of Breuer's "styleless" tubular-steel furniture designs espoused. The fact that the bottom of the frame was prow-shaped, and that the design actually moved, reinforced the imagery and added a note of wit to the design.

Fig. 79. Thonet tea cart B54, tubular steel, metal, and painted wood, 1929. The cart was originally manufactured with three spoked wheels; Thonet subsequently replaced the spokes with metal disks and later added a second front wheel.

Architectural Practice in Berlin 1928–31

As early as November 1926, Breuer had announced his intention to leave the Bauhaus once again. Nevertheless, Ise Gropius wrote in her diary, "The question of whether he will really leave remains open for the time being."[59] Breuer was not completely satisfied with his present situation, in which he increasingly found himself in conflict with other members of the school.

The central issue was Breuer's view that a designer should be able to design and carry out an entire project, from beginning to end. For example, he saw no reason why, in a Bauhaus project, the interior designer should have to relinquish responsibility for the color scheme to the wall-painting workshop. (Indeed, much of the conflict seemed to revolve around the differing opinions of architects versus painters, although it was often discussed in broader terms.) Breuer argued that the strict separation between departments in the school was ridiculous. And in a particularly animated debate on the subject, Breuer asserted that he was capable of handling all the details of any project; he could handle his commissions alone, and required no assistance. To many this signaled Breuer's complete rejection of the fundamental Bauhaus ideals of the cooperative artistic endeavor.[60]

As noted by Mrs. Gropius a few months later, Breuer

> says that he doesn't like the atmosphere any longer and that he would prefer to work alone in the future. His ambition prohibits him from tolerating the slightest bit of sub-

ordination, which cannot altogether be avoided when working in the large, communal team effort of the Bauhaus. The mood of the students is also partly critical of him. For G. [Gropius] a great loss, but Breuer's attitude of late has become so difficult that there is apparently no other way out.[61]

In 1927 he married a student, Marta Erps, and moved out of his Bauhaus quarters and into an apartment in the city of Dessau, thereby further distancing himself from the Bauhaus community.

Circumstances at the Bauhaus had indeed changed. There were conflicts between the formally oriented members of the faculty (e.g., Moholy-Nagy) and the more politically oriented (e.g., Hannes Meyer, who had been brought in by Gropius to head the new architecture department); Breuer placed himself in the camp of the formalists, publicly denouncing Meyer's emphasis on politics. There was also considerable pressure for the school to produce a larger number of commercially viable designs, which some teachers feared would turn the Bauhaus into "a vocational training school which evaluates only the final achievement and overlooks the development of the whole man."[62] Finally, outside criticism of the school was again on the rise.

In April 1927, Breuer, along with Herbert Bayer, formally submitted his resignation, effective in October. Breuer's motivations, finally, were more personal than philosophical. Even at so unusual a school as the Bauhaus, he felt overwhelmed by his teaching responsibilities and yearned to establish his own architectural practice. Bayer, for his part, wanted to reestablish a graphic-design business. Gropius urged them to stay on until the end of the term (spring 1928), and after some discussion, they agreed to do so. Ise Gropius noted in her diary: "At last an agreement with Breuer has been reached according to which he will stay at the Bauhaus. He will get to build an experimental house and also the affair with the metal chairs seems to have been settled."[63]

Much to everyone's surprise, Gropius himself resigned in January 1928. The Director's resignation was tendered because he felt that he was the real object of much of the recent criticism of the school, and also because he wanted to engage in independent architectural work, which his administrative responsibilities had made exceedingly difficult during the preceding years. Moholy-Nagy left the school a few days later, saying, "I can no longer keep up with the stronger and stronger tendency toward trade specialization in the workshops."[64] In mid-1928 Breuer moved to Berlin, where he established himself as an architect.

The unstable economic situation in Germany made it extremely difficult for most architects to find work, and by the end of 1928 Breuer's only designs that had been realized —aside from the design of his own apartment, which also served as his office—were for furniture. Like so many architects of the twenties, Breuer designed a number of large-scale projects that had little chance of realization. In 1928 and 1929 he designed large apartment buildings, hospitals, and a factory. In a way, Breuer was more fortunate than many of the older, more established architects, such as Gropius or Mies. He had an income from royalties on his tubular-steel furniture and was able to accept a number of small jobs which an architect of Gropius' stature might have turned down. Beyond that, he now lived a very modest bachelor's existence, his marriage having lasted only briefly.

INTERIORS

In 1929 Breuer began to design a number of significant interiors both for private clients and for several international exhibitions.

The unusual entrance hall and cloakroom of the Heinersdorff country house outside Berlin (fig. 80), the first of these, was extensively decorated with mosaic tile. The design was requested by the client and executed by his firm, Puhl-Wagner-Heinersdorff, which specialized in mosaic tile decoration. Breuer used tile as one element in a geometric composition of contrasting colors and surfaces. The unusual textures and geometry of the rooms could also be seen in a window (fig. 81) said to have been inspired by beer-mug bottoms and made from concave glass "lenses." The effect was of a multiple series of camera lenses, each with a slightly different view. Privacy was assured inside, while it was possible to glimpse, outside, a view made up of fragmented images.

Through Gropius, Breuer was commissioned in 1929 to design an apartment in Wiesbaden and an office in Mainz for Mr. Harnismacher, president of a large company making shoe-cleaning products. The spacious living room of the apartment (fig. 82) was provided with wooden furniture specially designed by Breuer. The color scheme — more typical of progressive Viennese interiors of the turn of the century than Germany of the 1920s — made use of a dark rug, dark trim, and contrasting wall colors articulating the various parts of the room. Lighting was hidden behind long, canted reflectors that lined the upper parts of the long walls. Although the study and dining room (fig. 83) lacked the decorative wall trim, the design of both rooms reflected a similar emphasis on precise geometry and simple and open spaces.

The one known room of the spacious office (fig. 84) was sparsely furnished, and brightly lit by the large picture window that filled one wall. The large desk with wooden top and thick tubular-steel legs would become the most common table used for dining rooms and

Fig. 80. Entrance hall and cloakroom, Heinersdorff country house, Berlin, 1929. A rare example of Breuer's use of geometric mosaic tile decoration.

studies in Breuer's interiors. It was used in a number of different shapes and sizes, adapted to the necessities of each commission. Cabinet units adapted from Breuer's original modular design of around 1926 were hung from the wall but were also supported from below. The room was unencumbered by massive or solid objects: the desk lacked solid drawer units and existed primarily on the horizontal plane; the chair was light and thin; and the bulk of the wall units was, for the most part, raised above the floor.

This conception of a free and open interior space was embraced by Breuer in all of his interiors at the time, including two arrestingly beautiful apartment designs of 1929 and 1930. The rooms that are known from contemporary photographs are nearly identical in plan.

The De Francesco apartment (figs. 85, 86), designed for a woman writer and critic, had a bedroom opening into a living-study-dining room. The same layout in the Boroschek apartment (fig. 87), commissioned by a stock broker and his wife, a singer, was used as a music room and dining room. In both cases the two rooms could be entirely closed off from one another, but the apartments were designed with the continuity and interaction of combined spaces foremost in mind.

In the De Francesco apartment, a band of modular wall cabinets made of shiny metal, glass, and wood, ran from one room to the next. Wall-to-wall woven oriental matting covered both floors, and the walls of both rooms were painted the same light, muted color. In addition to the long strip of hanging cabinets, the bedroom was furnished with a tubular steel bed, B35 lounge chairs, and a specially designed table with tubular-steel legs, lacquered top, and drawers beneath. A series of thin vertical wooden strips was applied to the wall behind the bed. These not only could be read as surface decoration, but served as an ingenious system for hanging prints or pho-

tographs, which could be inserted between or directly onto the strips. In the adjacent multipurpose room, the wall opposite the hanging cabinets was lined with bookshelves and storage shelves, from which projected a desk. At the far end of the room, by the window, were a couch and a dining table with chairs. Green plants, which Breuer described as "the best ornaments of all," were placed near the windows in both rooms.[65] The overriding impression of the De Francesco apartment was of openness, coolness, an almost steely minimal

Fig. 81. Multilens window, Heinersdorff house, Berlin, 1929. The unusual window was also exhibited at the 1930 Paris Salon des Artistes Décorateurs.

Fig. 82. Living room, Harnismacher apartment, Wiesbaden, 1929. The ebonized wood furniture and treatment of the walls were new elements in Breuer's interiors.

Fig. 83. Study and (in background) dining room, Harnismacher apartment, Wiesbaden, 1929. The study walls were lined with black lacquered wall units and bookshelves; both rooms were furnished with tubular-steel chairs and the recent table design sold by Thonet as B14, which Breuer used in virtually all of his subsequent interior designs.

quality, which was due in large part to the fact that the only contrasts in the light, monochromatic rooms were the punctuations of shiny tubular or flat nickel-plated steel. Despite its serenity, it was a disciplined and uncompromisingly modern design.

In contrast, the Boroschek apartment was eclectic, richer, and warmer. The Boroschek music room and dining room were painted different colors. The herringbone-laid polished wood floors were exposed and formed a background to brilliant, geometrically patterned oriental carpets. The strong horizontal line of wall units formed the visual link between the two rooms, just as in the De Francesco apartment, but here the treatment of the units was more varied. In the dining room (with the exception of two colored silverware drawers) the cabinets were painted to match the stark white of the wall from which they hung; in the music room they were painted a darker color than the tone used on the wall behind them. In addition, they served as a shelf on which the clients could display sculpture and handsome ceramic vases. At the end of the music room the line of cabinets was broken, terminating in two units that were lowered to form a fall-front desk and storage cupboard—a final grace note that neatly finished off the composition. The scheme provided a successful synthesis of the clients' taste for color, pattern, and opulent form and Breuer's usually narrow vocabulary of interior design. As Breuer stated:

> We have no desire for a purely formal point of view; instead we see our mission in creating a home that is simpler, lighter, more comfortable in the biological sense, and independent of exterior factors.[66]

Breuer's clients had to be completely predisposed to a modern aesthetic. Except for a few commissions where, somewhat against his wishes, Breuer was required to use traditional furnishings or decorative objects, the spaces he designed for his clients to live or work in were devoid of references to the past—either to the client's or to the history of interior architecture. In these interior designs,

Fig. 84. Harnismacher office, Mainz, 1929.

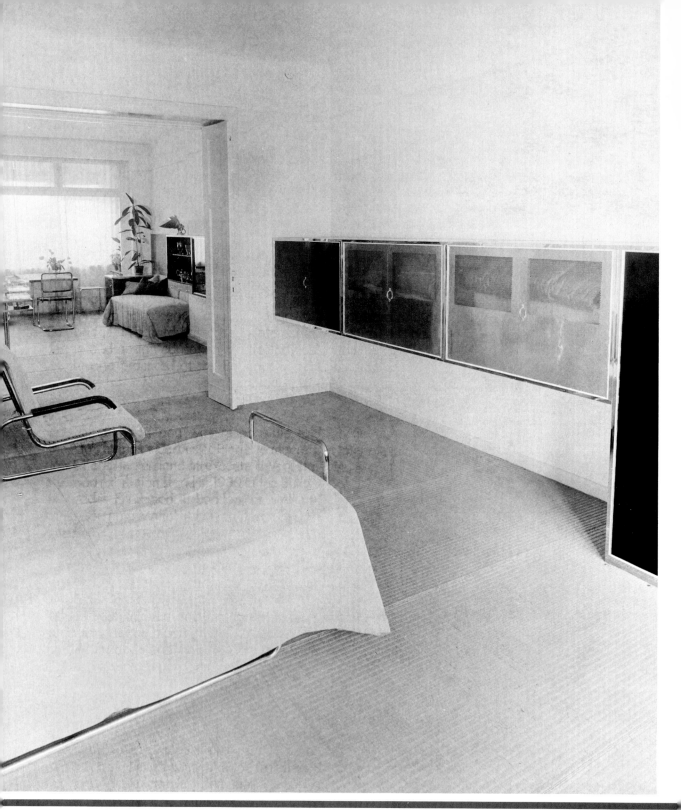

Fig. 85. Bedroom and study-living-dining room, De Francesco apartment, Berlin, 1929. The contrast of soft textures with hard, shiny surfaces and the clarity and precision of the entire scheme were characteristic of Breuer's finest interior designs.

Fig. 86. Bedroom, De Francesco apartment, Berlin, 1929. Shown is the system of vertical wooden strips for hanging pictures or photographs which Breuer had first used in his Berlin apartment the year before.

Fig. 87. Dining room and music room, Boroschek apartment, Berlin, 1930. Though somewhat more eclectic than the De Francesco apartment, this interior was equally effective. To the right of the door was a piano.

Breuer worked within a set of constraints far more rigid than those imposed on an architect beginning the design of a house. In most of Breuer's Berlin apartment renovations, he was largely prevented from altering the interior structure. His considerable talent enabled him to rise above these restrictions to create some of the most interesting and vital interiors of the period.

Around 1930 Breuer was hired by the psychologist Kurt Lewin and his wife Gertrude to remodel a Berlin house designed for the couple by the German architect Peter Behrens. Dr. Lewin, who was well on his way to becoming one of the giants of experimental psychology, was enthusiastic in his desire for a modern home. Behrens' early factory buildings (c. 1908–12) and product design had established the machine orientation of early modern architecture and design, and young architects like Gropius, Mies van der Rohe, and Le Corbusier received training in his office. In 1930 he was recovering from a prolonged illness and was attempting to revive his architectural practice; he was selected for the Lewin

house because of the relatively low fee he asked. After the house was designed the Lewins lost faith in Behrens because of numerous errors and eccentricities in the design — the original plans are said to have lacked a kitchen. Although the basic Behrens plans were retained, Breuer was hired to revise them and to design the interiors.

The living room was filled with furniture already in the clients' possession. The new rooms with modern furnishings were the dining room, study, and bedrooms. For the dining room (fig. 88) Breuer provided a large wall unit composed of sideboard, vitrine, and open shelving. Against an adjacent wall he placed a cabinet with special drawers for silver and linen, as well as storage space for related items. The cabinets were made of a light European maple in a natural lacquered finish; gray and clear glass shelves were used in the vitrine and on the table surface of the sideboard. The back of the exposed interior surface of the sideboard was faced in copper. The bases of all of the cabinet units were painted black; the walls of the dining room

Fig. 88. Dining room, Lewin house, Berlin, c. 1930. The photograph was taken shortly after the installation of the large, multipurpose wall unit.

were painted off white; the window curtains, which reached to the floor, were of ecru raw silk; and the floor was covered with oriental matting.

Dr. Lewin's study (figs. 89, 90) was lined with a new bookshelf system designed by Breuer. Although it was based on what must have been a commercial standard and bracket system, Breuer made the standards of shiny metal and the shelves of lacquered wood. At the end of each shelf were two lengths of tubular steel which served as bookends as well as stabilizers for the shelves. Continuous with the bookshelves on the long wall was a series of bright blue metal drawers specially assembled for notecards and papers, as well as additional shelf and cabinet space.

Furniture for the bedrooms consisted of a number of free-standing dressers, bedside tables and the like, executed in light cherry edged with ebonized wood. A desk for the master bedroom (fig. 91) was typical of the functional, geometrical forms that Breuer designed for the Lewin interiors. They possessed a monumentality and bulk that Breuer reserved for wooden cabinetwork. A low dressing chest (fig. 92), with a large shoe drawer that pivoted out from a hinge near the base, was placed below and to the side of a tall, thin dressing mirror—a scheme Breuer had used as early as 1925. The beds were tubular steel and the bedroom chairs were Thonet bentwood.

The work that Breuer did as an interior and furniture designer and architect received greatest recognition through the showing of his model interiors and projects at international exhibitions. His tubular-steel furniture in particular became the subject of much at-

Fig. 89. Bookshelf system, study, Lewin house, Berlin, c. 1930.

Fig. 90. Study, Lewin house, Berlin, c. 1930.

tention and discussion, at a time when he had all but ceased to design in tubular steel.

The appearance of a German section at the Paris Salon des Artistes Décorateurs in 1930 was an event that received extensive press coverage. Anti-German feeling had been strong in France since the end of the First World War and was responsible for the exclusion of German designers from the celebrated 1925 Paris Exposition Internationale des Arts Décoratifs et Industriels Modernes, where what little avant-garde design that had been permitted—Le Corbusier's Pavillon de l'Esprit Nouveau and Konstantin Melnikov's Pavilion of the U.S.S.R., for example—had been relegated to the outer edge of the exhibition. The 1925 Exposition had been dominated by the French, and, in particular, by such masters of the conservative Art Deco style as Emile-Jacques Ruhlmann, Süe et Mare, and Dufrêne.

When, four years later, the organizers of the 1930 Salon des Artistes Décorateurs invited the Deutscher Werkbund to send an exhibition of current German design, some eyebrows were raised; but much of the French design community, although unmoved by the intellectual rigor and austerity of the German work, realized that developments in Germany were far too important to be ignored any longer. The Salon was, in fact, the most solidly established and most conservative of the French artists' groups. A number of progressive designers, including Charlotte Perriand and René Herbst, had seceded to form their own organization, the Union des Artistes Modernes; their first exhibition was to be held shortly after that of the Artistes Décorateurs. This combination of circumstances made the appearance of the German designers all the more controversial.

Fig. 91. Desk, cherry and ebonized wood, for the Lewin house bedroom, Berlin, c. 1930. The consistently high quality of Breuer's cabinet-work can be attributed to his early education in carpentry and his interest in wood and its constructive possibilities.

The Deutscher Werkbund appointed Gropius to direct the exhibition, and Gropius selected his former Bauhaus colleagues Breuer, Moholy-Nagy, and Bayer as collaborators. Breuer not only designed an apartment space but also went to Paris to supervise the installation of the entire German section before the arrival of his colleagues.

The overall theme of the Werkbund section was mass-produced design in architecture, furniture, and household objects. The most spectacular part of the German exhibition was a suite of model rooms designed by Gropius and Breuer for Gropius' ten-story steel-frame apartment-building project, a model and drawings of which were also exhibited. Gropius designed a communal "club room" consisting of coffee bar, gymnastics and bathing areas, and a gallery with library and niches for reading, card playing, and listening to

Fig. 92. Dressing table-chest with mirror, cherry and ebonized wood, designed for the Lewin house bedroom, Berlin, c. 1930. Breuer's designs for dressing tables were always carefully combined with simple mirrors.

music. Gropius used Breuer's furniture throughout his spaces, although he himself designed the bar and high tables used between Breuer's lounge chairs. The structural framework of the exhibition space was steel, which was exposed and dramatically intensified by its nickel- or chrome-plated finish.

Immediately adjacent to the Gropius space was a series of model rooms designed by Breuer (figs. 93–96), which together represented a three-room unit in a residential hotel or boardinghouse. In fact, Breuer first conceived of the rooms for his own ten-story steel-framed apartment hotel, which he had designed in 1929 but which was never built.

The Breuer apartment consisted of a room for a woman (fig. 95) and one for a man (fig. 96), separated by a kitchenette and bath. Beyond the man's room was a study. The circulation path which visitors followed took them up the intricate steel staircase of the "bridge" Gropius had built between his and Breuer's spaces. From there they could get a bird's-eye view of Breuer's entire design from above (fig. 94), as if the roof had been removed from the building. Visitors then descended from the bridge and walked around the perimeter of the rooms as they entered and exited the other exhibition spaces; they were not permitted to walk into the model rooms.

Although the Breuer interiors appeared somewhat schematic to some visitors, because of the lack of actual ceilings and walls, they were specific and detailed in terms of furnishings and accessories.

Virtually one entire wall in each of the rooms consisted of windows with simple white shades. The opposite wall was fitted with hanging wall units as well as larger wardrobe cabinets, fronted with mirrors, which sat on the floor but were integrated with the wall units. Furniture in all rooms was Thonet tubular-steel designed by Breuer, plus a few file cabinets on casters and several specially designed pieces such as a cantilevered tubular-steel desk in the man's room and a pier table with semicircular glass top hung from a small, free-standing wall in the study. The man's room and woman's room differed only in the choices of colors for upholstery, rugs, linoleum, telephones, etc., and in the choice of accessories: flowers in the woman's room, globe and more bookshelf space in the man's. At the time of the exhibition Thonet had just begun large-scale production of tubular-steel furniture by Breuer and several French designers. Nine different Breuer designs were seen in the rooms or in an adjacent exhibition space where furniture was ingeniously installed by Herbert Bayer.

The effect of the German exhibition was profound. One writer referred to it as "the arrow pointing the way," and stated that "Henceforth the public decided to observe the development of metal furniture with sympathy."[67] The impressive work of each designer was lauded, as was cooperative effort.

> In all European countries, the same ideas have been advanced, the same efforts are being made. In our own country they are too dispersed. In Germany, they are more concentrated; artists and industrialists are working together in the same spirit. The Bauhaus at Dessau represents a whole generation of explorers capable of exploiting the numerous resources of modern technics; it is a school and a laboratory at the same time. Germany had realized the importance of the problem, which she has now considered in connection with the social readjustment now going on. And that is why, in the history of the industrial arts of the twentieth century, Germany will have the lion's share.[68]

The exhibition "Die Wohnung Unserer Zeit" (The Modern Home), part of the Berlin Bau-Ausstellung (Building Exhibition) of 1931, was intended as a "cultural demonstration and as a trade show," to present the state of modern architecture in Germany along with the newest

Fig. 93. Drawing, Apartment for a Boarding-house-Hotel, Deutscher Werkbund exhibition at the 1930 Paris Salon des Artistes Décorateurs. The disposition of the furniture was altered in the final installation of the Breuer rooms.

Fig. 94. Apartment for a Boardinghouse-Hotel, Paris exhibition, 1930. Photograph taken from the metal bridge separating the Gropius and Breuer rooms. From foreground to background: room for a woman, kitchenette and bathroom, room for a man, and beyond the elevated wall, the study.

97

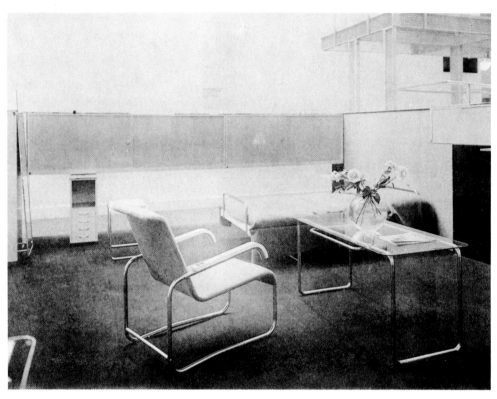

Fig. 95. Room for a Woman, Paris exhibition, 1930. Furnished with a B35 lounge chair, B19 table and desk, and specially designed bed and wall units.

Fig. 96. Room for a Man, Paris exhibition, 1930. Furnished with B25 lounge chair, B9 stool, B32 side chair, and specially designed cantilevered desk-tables. White pull shades covered the windows.

ideas in construction, city planning, and interior design. Several full-scale houses were built, and model interior spaces were also exhibited.

Breuer was not among the original group of architects invited to participate in the exhibition. As he explained years later:

> Mies and the others were angry because I was in Paris the year before, at the exhibition, and many others were not. I was, after all, a Hungarian, as Moholy was; Bayer was an Austrian, and Gropius was the only German in the German Pavilion.

But a few weeks before the opening, Mies called Breuer with an offer:

> Mies said, "Here is a space, you choose what you want to do and who you want to carry it off." I had to design it and carry it off myself with my own contractor…We opened in time, Mies didn't—he opened late.

Breuer, with the help of his former student and then assistant Gustav Hassenpflug, designed a "House for a Sportsman" (actually for a gymnastics teacher), showing it in plans (fig. 97), elevations (fig. 97), and a model interior (figs. 98–100); he also designed a "70 Square Meter Apartment."

Breuer was able to design and build his exhibition spaces so quickly because he made use of mass-produced furniture and elements (folding screens, oriental matting, gymnasium equipment) that could easily be ordered from suppliers. Even the wall units were based on earlier modular designs, and he had entrusted the plans to a Berlin cabinetmaker; the specified units were ordered over the telephone, and made of white maple (also called harewood).

The Sportsman's House, the program for which lent itself to open design and simple furnishing, was a large rectangle in plan. The interior was broken down into subsidiary functional spaces that could be separated from the larger sports or training room through the use of accordion doors. Standard Breuer bookshelves and wall units were used throughout, as was Thonet tubular-steel furniture.

Visitors entered the exhibition house in the sports room (fig. 98), near a wall with gymnasium equipment (no such entrance existed in the actual house plan). Facing the wall were the five small rooms, or "cabins"—a dressing room, bathroom, bedroom, study, and dining room. The last room against the far wall, the kitchen, as well as the second bathroom and the guest room, which all appeared in the plan, were suggested only by closed sliding doors. Most of the main room (fig. 99) served as the gymnasium or training space, although one corner was used as a living area (fig. 100). The informal and mobile nature of the living room was suggested by the casual arrangement of furniture and the use of the unusually thick gymnasium cushions as a sort of modular couch. Flexibility was the keyword in this design. The plan was open, but all spaces could be partitioned off when privacy was required. And even when the partitions to all five rooms against the wall were closed, communication between them was still possible, since the various cabinets and storage walls that served to divide them from each other stopped short of the far wall.

Breuer may have chosen the theme of the Sportsman's House because of ideas he was unable to carry out in an apartment for a sports teacher he had executed in Berlin the year before. This much-smaller apartment (fig. 101), located on the ground floor of a house, was divided into a gymnastics floor, through which visitors entered, and a minute living area, raised about a foot above it, which could be either combined or separated by a sliding, multisectioned wall. Fitted into the tiny living space were a desk and B34 armchair, a recessed sleeping alcove before which stood a B19 glass-topped dining table, a B3 club armchair, a B9 nesting stool, and a short wall of open metal bookshelves, behind which stairs led upward. In addition, doors led to a lavatory, storage closet, and a shower room, which also contained a sink and "cooking cabinet" (presumably enclosing a small stove or hot plate). The entire design was minimal, squeezed into the least possible space. And yet it did not give the impression of being on the one hand overcrowded or on the other austere. This was largely due to Breuer's sensitive use of materials—the elegant lightness of his metal-and-glass furniture and his decision to face the alcove (in which the couch sat) and the wall adjacent to it with richly figured wood veneers.

In the 1920s and '30s, the design of this type of minimal living space was the subject of particular concern to architects interested in mass-housing schemes, as well as to those who regarded the small programs as a design challenge. Breuer's "70 Square Meter Apartment" (figs. 102, 103), installed next to the Sportsman's House in the 1931 Berlin Bau-Ausstellung, was his own solution to the problem. This apartment was composed of sleeping niches, living area, wardrobe, bath, and kitchenette. It was furnished with beds, several chairs, a strip of wall units, a drawer unit, and two tubular-steel designs, both worked out well before the exhibition: a table and a couch. Breuer's 70 Square Meter Apartment, although minimal in its use of space, could not be considered a working-class dwelling because he included costly tubular-steel furniture, some of which was custom-made.

The essential ideas and vocabulary of Breuer's interior design were already present in his 1927 apartment for Piscator. But during the period 1928–31, especially in such projects as the De Francesco or Boroschek apartment, he emerged as an increasingly mature, confident, and sophisticated designer. There was a marked similarity in many of his interiors, especially in his repeated use of specific furnishings and materials. He deeply believed, for instance, in using the smallest possible number of well-chosen objects to do a job, and wrote that

> A few simple objects are enough, when these are good, multiuse and capable of variation. We avoid thus the lavish pouring of our needs into countless commodities that complicate our daily lives instead of simplifying them and making them easier.[69]

His use of a narrow range of furniture was tied to a conception popular among progressive architects and designers at the time—that only a few standardized furniture types (*Typenmöbel*) were necessary to fulfill many and varied uses. Separate desks and dining tables, for example, were discarded in favor of a well-designed table that could function as both. A bed could serve as a couch. As Breuer put it: "One can design it so that it provides seating and lounging space during the day—which also eliminates the need for extra chairs."[70] Chairs themselves should be lightweight and easily movable so that they can fulfill various functions. A wall unit could store books or glassware, clothes or art objects; it could also divide or create interior spaces. In Breuer's interiors the emphasis was always on the form and on adapting it to as many uses as possible. And although Breuer was willing to design one-of-a-kind pieces of furniture for affluent clients, most of his work concentrated on the use of versatile, mass-produced furnishings. His fondness for oriental matting, which during this period appeared in many of his interiors, was not due solely to the beauty of its soft, natural color and its unique texture, but also to the fact that it was less expensive than ordinary carpeting and could be rolled up easily for cleaning. His ideas on the freeing of floor space dictated his use of thin and transparent furniture or built-in furniture hung from the wall. And his strictly utilitarian view of lighting meant that

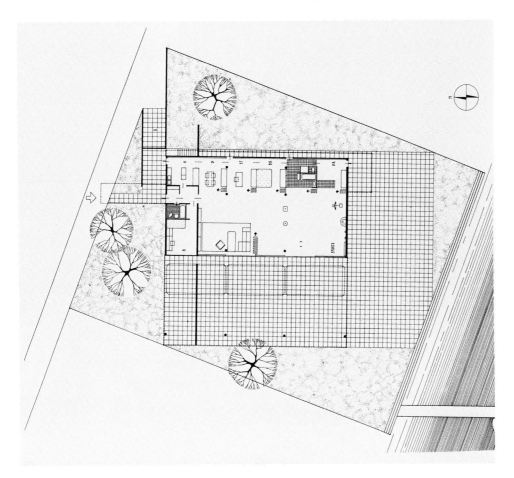

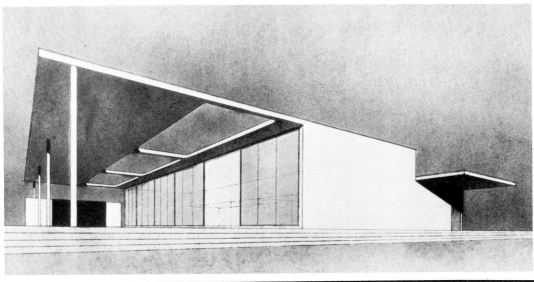

Fig. 97. Plan and elevation, Sportsman's House, Berlin Bau-Ausstellung, 1931. Breuer's exhibition house reflected the continuing vogue for physical fitness.

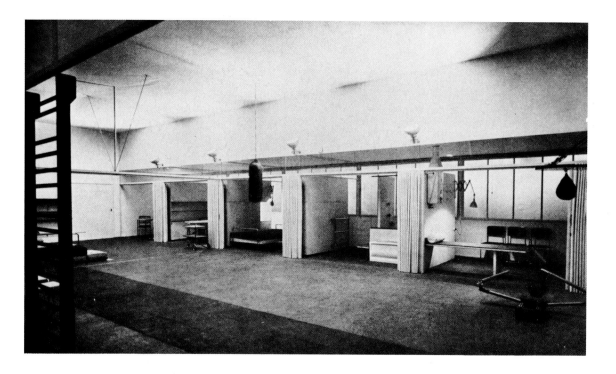

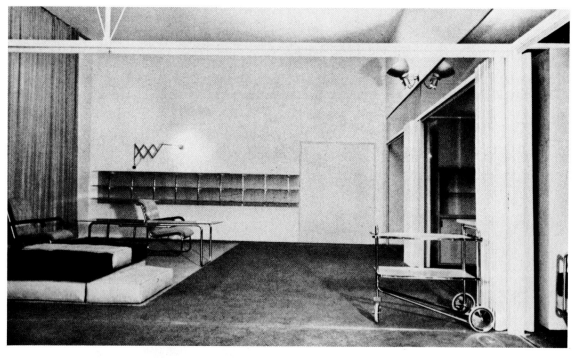

Fig. 98. Sportsman's House, Berlin Bau-Ausstellung, 1931. View into the exhibition interior showing the five living spaces, or "cabins", and the large gymnasium floor.

Fig. 99. Sportsman's House, Berlin Bau-Ausstellung, 1931. View into "living room", which could be separated from the gymnasium area by closing the folding wall. To the right stood Breuer's B54 tea cart.

in most commissions he made use of the same desk lamps and industrial reflectors.

Breuer's use and reuse of these various elements did not result in monotony or mindless repetition. He saw no need to rework or reinterpret his ideas merely for the sake of novelty. His ideas (some might say his formula) worked well, and they led him to design many of the most interesting and vital interiors of the period.

FURNITURE

During his years in Berlin, Breuer designed several examples of seating furniture which, although clearly intended for production, were never mass-produced. One of the most interesting chairs, yet little known, was designed for the 1929 Harnismacher apartment (fig. 82) and was also used in the 1932 Harnismacher house (fig. 108). This chair, basically a cube, was formed out of arms of laminated wood bent to form squares with rounded

corners, connected at the front and back by wooden stretchers. Between the arm units a canvas seat and pivoting back were stretched between tubular-steel rods. The chair was probably designed as part of a set, with a simple geometrical wooden coffee table and couch of ebonized wood and cane (fig. 82). These designs reflected Breuer's interest in bentwood (and cane), which he had already used in his B32 and B64 chairs (figs. 71, 72), designed the year before. The "cube chair" was a form that had fascinated designers, because of its potential for geometric abstractions, since at least the turn of the century, and such architects as Josef Hoffmann, Koloman Moser, Frank Lloyd Wright, and Le Corbusier had already tried their hand at it. Most of them, however, had chosen to interpret the cube as a solid, filling it with soft cushions confined within the hard frame. Breuer's design—typically for his work of this period—played on the idea of transparency; in this it

Fig. 100. Living room, Sportsman's House, Berlin Bau-Ausstellung, 1931.

Fig. 101. Apartment for a Gymnastics Teacher, Berlin, 1930. View into the small living space of the apartment, photographed from above a desk placed against one wall; to the left was the gymnastics floor, to the right the sleeping alcove.

Fig. 102. 70 Square Meter Apartment, Berlin
Bau-Ausstellung, 1931. The multipurpose use
of standardized furniture types (chairs, tables,
bed-couches) was demonstrated in the minimum dwelling, where each item of furniture
had to fulfill a number of different functions.

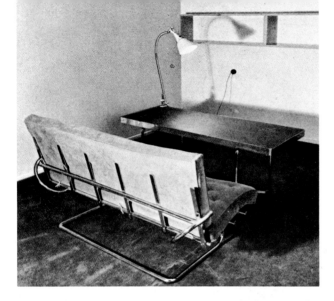

Fig. 103. Couch, tubular steel and flat steel bars with upholstered cushions, 1930–31. The original version as exhibited in the 70 Square Meter Apartment at the Berlin Bau-Ausstellung (top) and a replica built in 1981 (bottom). (Replica collection The Museum of Modern Art, gift of Lily Auchincloss. © 1981 The Museum of Modern Art, New York; all rights reserved.)

was not unlike his first tubular-steel chair, the club armchair.

The tubular-steel couch (fig. 103) Breuer included in the 1931 Berlin Bau-Ausstellung was, in all likelihood, not specifically designed for the exhibition, but was instead a project that he had been working on for some time. (In view of the short notice which Breuer said he was given to prepare his section of the exhibition, it would have been impossible to construct even a prototype of the couch.) Although the entire structure of the couch is difficult to see in surviving photographs, it is clear that the frame was made from both tubular and flat steel bars. As in most Breuer designs, the steel frame and the upholstered seat and back were independently articulated. Separate tufted rectangular seat and back cushions were tied to the frame. The structural skeleton of the back, including the round tubes that extended from the sides, was exposed and became, in fact, the most striking element in the couch's aesthetic. The couch was exhibited as a free-standing object, and so important was its back that it seems likely Breuer had no intention of its ever being used conventionally against a wall.

Breuer's last tubular-steel chair was designed in 1931 but never produced in any form. A part of his project for the Kharkov Theater in Russia, the chair (fig. 104), as well as the building itself, was strongly influenced by Russian avant-garde design. In an unusual graphic technique, Breuer superimposed a drawing of the seating planned for the theater onto his plans for the building. The seating was made up of rows of rotating tubular-steel chairs with wooden or upholstered seats and backs. The freedom of the design and the emphasis on curving lines were reminiscent of Vladimir Tatlin's 1927 cantilevered chair, which was published in 1931. The design was quite unlike anything else Breuer produced at this or any time in his career.

Fig. 104. Seating for the Kharkov Theater, U.S.S.R., 1931. Breuer's proposed chairs, as well as the theater itself, were heavily influenced by the forms of Russian Constructivism.

Travels and Design Work 1931–34

By November 1931 Breuer had left Berlin. Although he maintained the lease on his apartment and sublet it, never again would the German capital be his permanent place of residence. Between 1932 and late 1935, Breuer's homes would always be temporary. In his letters from those years he wrote of moving to other cities, or waiting, hopefully, for a given project to be accepted or built. Much of early 1932 and a large part of 1933 were spent traveling. Subsequently he divided his time, for the most part, between Budapest and Zurich.

His first trip, which he undertook with great zeal in his beloved Ford automobile (which also served as his mobile office), led him through France, where he saw new Corbusier buildings, including the De Mandrot house, and to Spain. From Spain he traveled along the Mediterranean and also to North Africa; eventually he visited Greece with Herbert Bayer, his occasional traveling companion and good friend. During these trips he became increasingly enthralled with the forms of vernacular building, and in 1934 he attempted to explain the spiritual kinship between ''vernacular architecture and the Modern Movement.''

> …these two diametrically opposed tendencies have two characteristics in common: the impersonal character of their forms; and a tendency to develop along typical, rational lines that are unaffected by passing fashions.[71]

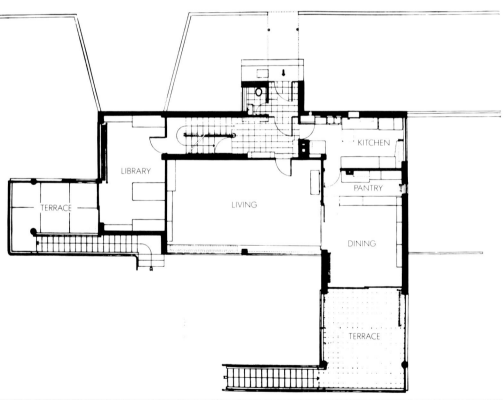

LIBRARY

TERRACE

LIVING

KITCHEN

PANTRY

DINING

TERRACE

Fig. 105. Harnismacher house, Wiesbaden, 1932. Breuer's first house design to be built was located in a corner of its site, oriented toward the large garden. The contrast with the adjoining houses was startling.

Fig. 106. Plan of the first floor, Harnismacher house, Wiesbaden, 1932.

109

He saw in vernacular architecture characteristics that others might have had difficulty recognizing. And although the basis of his interest lay in a deep affection for the forms, he explained it in terms of their strictly rational development, which "ultimately standardizes them as type-forms."

HARNISMACHER HOUSE

While in the south Breuer received word that his former client Harnismacher had finally decided to build a house in Wiesbaden, near Frankfurt. Breuer designed the house probably during June 1932. Construction was begun in July and completed by December. Although he first returned briefly to Berlin, he spent at least the summer in Wiesbaden working on the house.

At the age of thirty, seven years after beginning his professional career in design, Breuer was given the opportunity to build his first entirely new, free-standing house. The completed house (figs. 105–09) was widely published, a fact which Breuer modestly attributed to the general paucity of building in Europe at the time.

The Harnismacher house was a three-story villa, each floor of which was organized differently. Its basic vocabulary was Corbusian, but certain structural devices, the use of contrasting materials, and the distinctive interiors were completely Breuer's. It was sited on a hill, and the street side was only two stories high and had few windows, while the principal facade was to the south, facing the garden. The house was a steel-frame and concrete structure faced with whitish-gray stucco to which fine pieces of basalt were added to provide a more textured surface; the exterior staircases were reinforced concrete; the projecting terrace walls were of smooth asbestos sheeting;

Fig. 107. Living room, Harnismacher house, Wiesbaden, 1932. Tubular steel and black lacquered wood furniture were juxtaposed with the white walls and light linoleum floors.

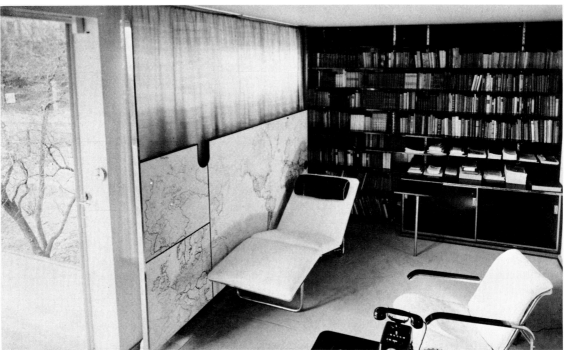

Fig. 108. Wall unit and armchair, living room, Harnismacher house, Wiesbaden, 1932.

Fig. 109. Library, Harnismacher house, Wiesbaden, 1932. Somewhat secluded on a wing of the house which stood between the first and second stories, accessible by a separate staircase, the study was furnished with black lacquered shelves and wall units and with a reclining chair from the 1929 apartment.

and the garden retaining walls were of rough fieldstone. This combination of widely varying materials would characterize Breuer's architecture through the rest of his career.

The east walls of the terrace, which faced the nineteenth-century mansion next door, were made of frosted glass. These terraces, braced with "nautical cables and marine hardware," together with the strong horizontal lines, strip windows, and clean whiteness, lent a Mediterranean feel and nautical imagery to the house, qualities it shared with the work of leading modernist architects of the period.

The furnishings of the first- and second-floor living spaces—the ground floor contained a garage and service area—were, for the most part, taken from the apartment Breuer had designed for the Harnismachers in 1929. The central and largest space of the first floor was the living room (figs. 107, 108), one entire wall of which was given over to large metal-framed picture windows overlooking the garden. The detailing of this window wall was precisely studied; the continuous metal gratings added the shine and patterning of metal to the shelf surface. The interior walls were painted white, while most of the wooden furniture or trim was finished in polished black. Sharp contrast of the various finishes and materials within the bright and unencumbered space was the main device used to achieve the elegant and subdued effect of the room, as it was in other parts of the house—which were not, unfortunately, well photographed.

SWITZERLAND

Toward the end of 1932, Breuer began to spend more time in Zurich, where, through his friendship with Sigfried Giedion, he obtained several important commissions. The first of these was the redesign of the Wohn-

Fig. 110. Wohnbedarf store, Basel, 1933. Breuer renovated the facades and interiors of the Wohnbedarf stores, and Herbert Bayer designed the catalogs and other graphics.

bedarf stores in Zurich and Basel. Wohnbedarf was one of the first modern home-furnishings stores devoted to the selling of the latest architect-designed furniture and accessories. Founded by Giedion, Werner Moser, and Rudolf Graber, all then associated with the Swiss Werkbund, the store sold the furniture of Breuer, Corbusier, Alvar Aalto, Max Bill, and Moser, among others. Breuer was asked to renovate the stores, which were to be showcases of the new interior design. Both stores had large street-level windows to draw people into the store. The facade of the Basel branch (fig. 110) was designed to appear as if it had been cut out of a huge panel of corrugated metal. The interior of the Zurich store (fig. 111) was a large, open space, divided by structural pillars and punctuated with various hanging elements and ensembles of furniture. Photographs of modern buildings, draperies, and grass-mat screens, as well as lighting fixtures hung from

the ceiling, offered themselves for purchase while also serving to break up the space. One wall was fitted with Breuer's vertical-strip system for hanging photographs and became itself an additional textured surface in the room. A steel-railinged mezzanine was constructed for additional display space, devoted mostly to model rooms or furniture ensembles. It could be reached by a dynamic Breuer staircase with cantilevered steps that boldly projected into the room, a sculptural object worthy of attention. This type of staircase became one of the most common features of Breuer's later houses and interiors. The design of the store provided a bright and open space that served as the perfect backdrop for the selling of the store's wares.

The association with Giedion led Breuer to codesign, with the Swiss architects Alfred and Emil Roth, the Doldertal flats (figs. 112, 113) in Zurich. The apartment buildings were built by

Fig. 111. Wohnbedarf store, Zurich, 1933. The projecting sculptural staircase would become one of the most typical and outstanding features of Breuer's later houses.

Giedion on property belonging to his family, in order to provide financial security that would allow them to maintain their own house on the grounds. Design and redesign of the project stretched over several years, and, because of extensive problems with buildings permits, construction was not begun until 1934.

The pair of four-story apartment blocks were well sited on a hill, and the flats were designed to make living in an apartment as much as possible like living in a house. The ground floors were given over to garage and storage spaces and servants' rooms; and although the plan and number of apartments varied on each of the other three floors, each building contained a total of five apartments. Ample terrace space was provided for all. Developing ideas first employed in the Harnismacher house, Breuer, along with the Roths, used the awnings and shutters to best aesthetic advantage. The design of the houses, and of the apartments, was striking and effective.

The single-floor apartments (fig. 113) were planned with a large, open living-dining area at one end of the apartment and a large master bedroom with dressing area at the other, both with wide expanses of window. The spaces, furnished by the architects, had wooden floors covered with soft woven rugs and expanses of light-colored wall hung with an occasional wall unit. Most of the furniture used was designed by either Breuer or Alvar Aalto, whose furniture designs were becoming increasingly popular. They reflected not only the collaborative nature of the project, but the wider, less-rigorous vocabulary of Breuer's interiors after 1933.

WOHNBEDARF FURNITURE

In addition to the Wohnbedarf stores, Breuer designed, or redesigned, a group of furniture items that were marketed beginning in 1933. These included a bookcase (fig. 114), a desk

Fig. 112. Breuer with Alfred and Emil Roth, Doldertal flats, Zurich, 1934. This was one of the most successful and widely published schemes for small modern apartment houses. The flats were constructed from a steel frame and concrete.

(fig. 114), a set of tables, and several pieces of aluminum furniture.

Breuer had designed a number of bookcases, but the one designed for Wohnbedarf, made of tubular-steel frame and wooden shelves, was a free-standing unit, intended for use alone or in combination with identical models. Each set of shelves was supported by and raised up on a pair of two-footed tubular-steel bases, to which were attached a pair of upright shafts of tubular steel. The lengths of steel were inserted through each shelf, the top shelf sitting atop the lengths of tube. The desk was a design variant of a scheme Breuer had been using since 1926. His conception of a well-designed desk consisted of a drawer unit on the left, a simple rectangular tabletop, and a tubular-steel support on the right. To Breuer the formula seemed perfect and uncomplicated, and he seldom found reason to approach the design from a different point of view.

Another redesign was a series of tables Breuer produced for Wohnbedarf similar to Thonet's B14 and to other of his earlier tables (figs. 84, 87). They were sold as the optimum solution to the mass-produced table, appropriate for dining or study, and combinable so that smaller and larger tables could be used together for large gatherings.

ALUMINUM FURNITURE, 1932–34

The Breuer designs which Wohnbedarf eventually sold in greatest quantity, and for which the firm was exclusive agent in Switzerland, were a line of aluminum furniture designed in 1932 and marketed beginning in 1933. These designs were intended for construction in materials less costly than the twenty-five-millimeter nickel- or chrome-plated tubular steel then being used in the manufacture of cantilevered tubular-steel chairs. Although Breuer specified that the chair frames were to be "preferably constructed of bands of metal,

Fig. 113. Apartment interior, Doldertal flats, Zurich, 1934. All of the furniture was from Wohnbedarf, for the most part designed by Breuer or Aalto.

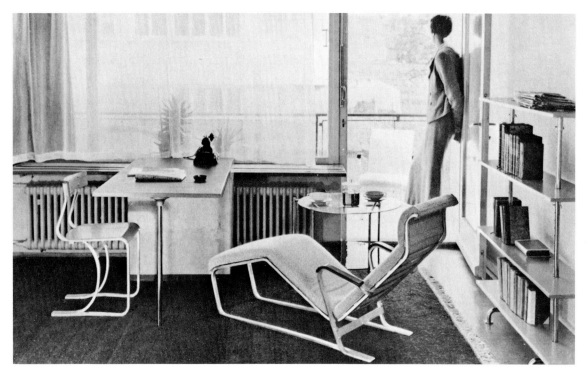

wood, or artificial material or a combination of these," the drawings show a large number of chairs in tubular steel (figs. 115, 116).[72] Here, however, the tubular steel was to be a thinner, lesser-quality one, and the band metal Breuer had most in mind was aluminum.

It has long been thought that the aluminum designs originated with Breuer's participation in an international competition for aluminum chairs held in Paris in November 1933. This was, however, not the case. Breuer made his first designs in mid-1932, and sought protection by applying for a patent and design registration in Germany in November 1932. By the time of the competition in November 1933, Breuer had signed contracts for the production of his furniture with four companies: Embru-Werke A.G. in Switzerland, L. & C. Arnold G.m.b.H. in Germany, Stylclair in France, and A. L. Colombo in Italy. He had aggressively sought manufacturers in virtually every European country and by 1934 had contracted for

production with the Société Industrielle d'Ameublement (S.I.D.A.M.)' in Belgium and was negotiating with Induventa in Holland, Luminium Ltd in England, and later with Artek in Finland.

The "International Competition of the Best Aluminum Chair" was sponsored by the Alliance Aluminium Cie of France, which sought to promote the use of aluminum as a material for furniture production. Designers from fourteen countries entered 209 chair designs, 54 of which were executed in prototype form. Breuer was persuaded to enter the competition by the Embru company, which manufactured the five models sent to the competition and covered all expenses. Two independent juries judged the competition, offering separate prizes. The first consisted of five representatives of the aluminum industry. The second was selected from the delegates to the International Congress of Modern Architecture (C.I.A.M.). Among the latter jury were Sigfried

Fig. 114. Breuer furniture shown in the Swiss Werkbund's "Neubühl" housing development, 1932. The aluminum chairs manufactured by Embru and desk and bookshelf by Wohnbedarf were all marketed by Wohnbedarf beginning in 1933.

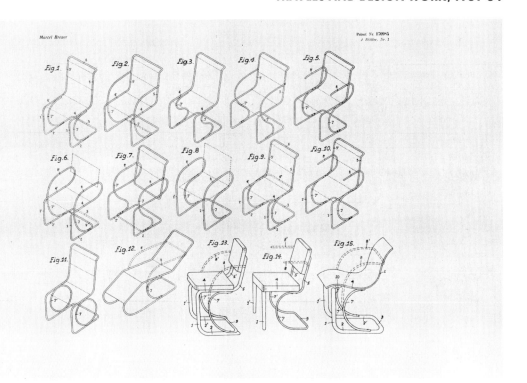

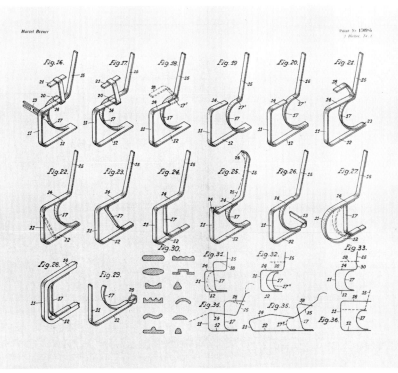

Fig. 115. Swiss patent drawing, "Frames for Springy Chairs," filed 31 October 1933 but identical with the German patent filed in November 1932.

Fig. 116. Second page of Swiss patent drawings. The designs were intended for production in "bands of metal, wood, or artificial materials or a combination of these."

Giedion, Walter Gropius, and, according to some accounts, Le Corbusier. The industry group met first and unanimously selected the Breuer designs as the first-prize winner. The second jury, which awarded its prize in the name of the C.I.A.M., also chose Breuer unanimously. Breuer's chairs were seen by the judges as highly original conceptions that took greatest advantage of the intrinsic qualities of the material. Most of the other entrants designed chairs that were translations into aluminum of typical tubular-steel or wooden chairs of the period. The band-metal furniture seemed destined to become Breuer's most successful furniture project to date, with the unusual promise of financial reward that had hitherto eluded him. The unanimous awarding of the first prize in the Paris competition seemed only to enhance the possibilities for success. By the time the first mass-produced Breuer aluminum and band-steel chairs had been put on the market in 1934, they had already been extensively published in architectural and design periodicals.

Aluminum was not, however, at the time, a particularly popular material for furniture design. It was considered too inflexible and brittle for use in furniture production and too expensive for the marketplace. Although some commercial aluminum furniture was made in Europe and, to a greater extent, in the United States, it was by no means common; and it was virtually unheard of in the domestic interior. Breuer's designs were among the first to lead to a reconsideration of aluminum as a suitable material for furniture.

The aluminum Breuer chose for use in his chairs was a hard, nonoxidizing alloy with a particularly high resistance to corrosion. According to Breuer it was the hardest available at the time. The specific alloy was called simply "anticorodal," or anticorrosive. The use of such a nonrusting material would allow chairs to be used outdoors and in wet or humid climates—an advantage that set the new furniture apart from nickel- or chrome-plated tubular-steel furniture, which was far more susceptible to rusting.

A further desirable characteristic of aluminum was its light weight. Breuer claimed that an aluminum chair would weigh less than half as much as a similar tubular-steel chair. This became a strong selling point since it meant that aluminum furniture could be much more cheaply shipped and would be far easier to handle. This was especially the case for the long reclining chairs. The material was unusually malleable and therefore relatively easy to work with. In its alloy form it was also flexible and resilient. An appealing feature of aluminum, and in particular of the alloy used in the Breuer chairs, was its silverlike appearance. The surface did not require plating with nickel or chrome and could be manufactured with either a glossy or dull finish. Many contemporary descriptions refer to the "flat-matte" or "dull-silver" finish of the surface.[73]

The material's only real disadvantage for use in furniture, in fact, when compared to tubular steel, was the fact that it is not nearly as strong. The use of aluminum therefore dictated a more complex structural system for the chair. The simple cantilever of the tubular-steel chair had to be replaced by a new system of auxiliary supports.

THE CHAIR DESIGNS

In his new aluminum designs Breuer's main concern was to construct a chair that would have a second or auxiliary set of supports (in addition to the front legs) rising from the ground member to add stability to the seat, and, in certain designs, form the arms and/or back of the chair (figs. 115, 116). A noncantilevered tubular-steel chair could easily be made from tubing 20 percent thinner. Accordingly, fifteen of the patented designs refer to tubular steel. Of those, probably only one model was eventually manufactured (fig. 117), and that only in small quantity. The appeal of the chair, manufactured by S.I.D.A.M. in Belgium, was limited. Its close similarity to standard tubular-steel cantilevered chairs, on the market for five or six years, made its selling potential limited. And without large-scale production, the hoped-for low price could scarcely become a reality.

Breuer saw the main application of his new designs to less costly "bands of metal, wood, or artificial material or a combination of these materials."[74] Since, however, unlike tubular steel, some of these materials could not be either easily welded or riveted, Breuer's newly patented construction called for a wide band of material to be slit along its length and the different pieces bent into separate parts.

One of the combined models mentioned in the patent was made in prototype form (fig. 118). Breuer, with Embru, made a chair whose seat, front legs, and ground members were made of bent plywood, while the rear supports and back frame were made from two continuous pieces of aluminum, joined by a brace below the seat. The awkwardness of the design, despite its lower cost due to the limited use of metal, must have dissuaded any manufacturer from producing the chair.

The aluminum bands used for these new chairs were cast in a rectangular shape but grooved-out so that the profile formed a double inverted U-shape from side to side (fig. 124, upper right). The full width was used only at the rear of the base; once the band was split into the front and back vertical members, the section of each was a single inverted U. Where the band became the support for the seat, the U was filled in with a specially cast piece of metal, in order to accept the rivets that were

Fig. 117. Experimental prototype of aluminum, wood, and cane side chair, made by Breuer with the Embru company in Switzerland, 1932–33.

Fig. 118. Experimental prototype of tubular-steel side chair, 1932–33. Apparently made in Belgium by S.I.D.A.M., a licensee of Breuer's designs.

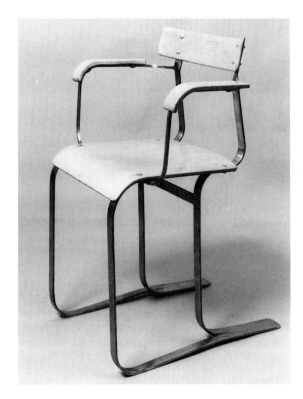

required to attach the wooden or metal seat slats. In the original patent designs (fig. 116) Breuer illustrated a number of different possible profiles for the sections of metal. Among the reasons given for the grooved-out shape of the material was that it could thereby "accept ornamentation or bars."[75] In another context Breuer suggested inserting rubber strips into the grooves at the base to prevent any possible scratching of floors or discoloration of carpets.[76]

Most of the designs in Breuer's patent, and all but two of the chair designs eventually produced, were for upright side or armchairs. Two lounge-chair designs and two variations on a nesting table model were also manufactured.

There were three basic side-chair designs, all of which also came in armchair versions. The aluminum frames of all three were quite similar, although there were variations in size, proportion, and materials offered for the seats

and backs. Model 301 (fig. 119), as it was designated in the Wohnbedarf catalog, was the smallest and least expensive. It was sold with a molded-plywood seat and back for use in cafés, restaurants, and offices, and as model 305 with slatted wood seat and back for gardens and terraces. Both chairs came in armchair versions and were also available with frames made of thin bands of steel, a less costly material than aluminum.

Model 303 (fig. 120) was slightly larger, made with a more fully articulated back and with wooden-framed caned seat and back, for use in restaurants, living rooms, and dining rooms.

Model 307, the largest of these designs, came with upholstered seat and back and was intended for use in the home. Neither the upholstered nor caned model was available in plain band metal, which was considered unsuitable for domestic use.

Compared with Breuer's earlier cantilevered chairs, the lines of these new chairs were less strictly geometrical. Emphatic curves, introduced into the auxiliary support members beneath the seat and into the shape of the back support, fulfilled an important structural function; not only did they provide much-needed support, but they also gave the chair a greater degree of resilience. In all of the designs, the pieces of cast aluminum began at the rear of the base and split into two pieces. One piece continued along the ground, forming the base, and rose to become the front leg and main part of the seat frame; the other rose to form the curved auxiliary support and then continued up to form the back. In none of the final production versions of the chair did the supporting elements rise above to form an arm. Rather, the arm was an independent appendage attached to the underside of the seat or seat frame and to the back.

Breuer's aluminum chairs were among the lightest metal chairs of the period. They were also unusually flexible and comfortable. The

Fig. 119. Wohnbedarf model 301, band steel and wood, 1932–33. (Collection Manfred Ludewig, Berlin.) Breuer's aluminum and band-steel side chairs and armchairs were distinguished for their lightness, flexibility, and comfort.

problematic aspects of these designs rested in the fact that the addition of the auxiliary supports (and of separate arms) and the shapes of the backs made the chairs look squat and compacted. The designs seemed busy, giving the impression that a great deal of material, with straight lines crowded next to curved lines, had been compressed into too little space.

Such was emphatically not the case, however, with Breuer's aluminum lounge chairs (figs. 121, 124, 125). Those designs achieved a structural and aesthetic solution that resulted in furniture of genuine originality, comfort, and refinement.

Like Breuer's side chairs and armchairs, the lounge models were conceived as cantilevered structures with additional supports. The cru-

cial difference in the lounge chairs was that the seat was both suspended between and held up by the arms, which were the main load-bearing element of the design. In these models the expression of the cantilever became an emphatic statement, the crucial element within the design. The cantilever that resulted from the continuous lengths of aluminum forming the ground members, front legs, and seat and back frame on each side was so extreme that the chair would collapse without the additional support given by the arms. Its treatment was critically different from that in the other designs because of the degree of freedom with which the seat was allowed to move, both vertically and horizontally, as it hung from the arms. This suspended structure

Fig. 120. Wohnbedarf model 303, aluminum, wood, and cane, 1932–33.

Fig. 121. Lounge chair, aluminum and wood,
1932–33. (Collection The Museum of Modern
Art, gift of the designer.) Although it was one
of Breuer's most remarkable designs, it shared
one inexplicable characteristic with the later
Isokon lounge chairs: the small scale of the
design. Neither the aluminum chairs nor the
Isokon lounge chairs would accommodate a
person of average size.

allowed considerable lateral movement, which was unusual but not in any way the result of a structural defect; rather, it represented a deliberate effort to make the chair feel as flexible and comfortable as possible. Further, the suspension of the sitter within the frame was clearly and simply articulated. The result for the sitter was a design of visual clarity and physical comfort.

Breuer's talent for careful detailing in his furniture was demonstrated by several aspects of the aluminum reclining chairs. Part of the beauty of the designs stemmed from the fact that the two pieces which began as one at the base and split apart to form the frame of the chair were designed to follow parallel lines: the overall shape of the base/arm piece directly mirrored that of the lower part of the frame (base/front legs and seat). That the angle of the arm was identical to the angle of the seat was not a structural necessity, nor was it always the choice made in his armchairs—for example, in the first tubular-steel club armchair. The original model for the reclining chair, shown at the competition, had a completely different shape (fig. 122): there the arm support was completely rounded as it descended from the back to the floor.

A more unusual element was the twist that the aluminum bar was given behind the wooden armrest (figs. 121, 125). This element was an idiosyncratic feature with a very distinct function: it was added to give resilience and strength to the member. The turning or twisting of the material added strength to the arm at a critical stress point; the twist diffused the load applied to the back part of the arm. In the original patent drawing, Breuer used it only at the base of a chair, where extra support and resilience were desired. In production models of the thinner band-steel chairs, the arm was twisted on both sides of the armrest. In the aluminum chairs, including the variant shown at the Paris competition (fig.

122), it was used only behind the armrest, where the planar orientation of the aluminum surfaces had to be shifted forty-five degrees in order to attach the arm to the back of the chair. Other ways could have been devised to attach the arm to the chair back. Despite its structural rationale, the twist can be seen as a very elegant and successful aesthetic feature of the design. Breuer even used the twist at the base of a desk design where resilience was not an issue and where the need for additional support was negligible. This element bore testimony to the loosening of Breuer's design vocabulary, away from the strict geometry of Bauhaus-oriented design.

Breuer designed long and short versions of this lounge chair, which was available in aluminum or band steel, with upholstery for indoor use, waterproof upholstery for outdoor use, or with a wooden slat seat for outdoors. (The upholstered versions had flat metal slats spanning the sides of the frame.) The only variation between the longer and shorter versions of the chairs was the shape of the headrest. On the long chair it was higher and more

Fig. 122. Short lounge chair, steel and wood, 1932–33. This experimental version was identical with the model shown at the Paris competition in November 1933. (Collection Technische Hogeschool, Afdeling der Bouwkunde, Delft, Netherlands.)

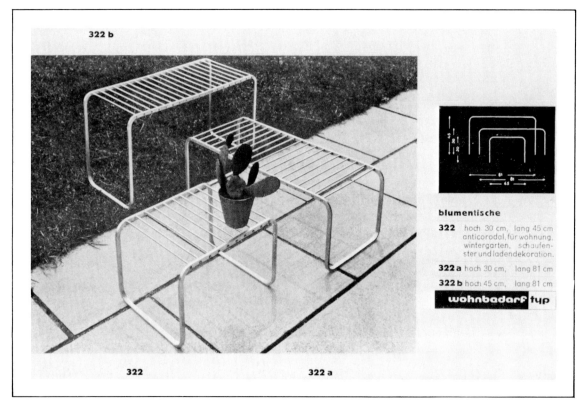

322 b

blumentische

322 hoch 30 cm, lang 45 cm
anticorodal, für wohnung,
wintergarten, schaufen-
ster und ladendekoration.

322 a hoch 30 cm, lang 81 cm

322 b hoch 45 cm, lang 81 cm

wohnbedarf typ

322   322 a

emphatically contoured to the sitter's neck and back, while the short chair had a simple straight back; for an additional charge, however, the more delicately shaped headrest was available on either the aluminum or steel models of the short chair.

The final aluminum designs were two tables. The first, a set of four nesting tables, was a translation of Breuer's Bauhaus tubular-steel stools into aluminum with rectangular cross section. The only difference was that the wooden tops were attached to the top of each metal member, rather than being inserted between the side members.

He also designed a set of three flower or garden tables (fig. 123). These were not nesting tables, but were made in different sizes from the same rectangular-sectioned aluminum. Their tops were made of aluminum rods. The tables were advertised as being suitable for living

rooms, winter gardens, windows, and store decoration. They were also occasionally used as magazine racks.

As happened so often to Breuer, the early promise of commercial success these designs seemed to hold did not materialize. Despite the many contracts and advances he held for the production of the chairs, only Embru and Wohnbedarf in Switzerland were able to make a success of manufacturing and selling the designs. All of the other contracts were eventually terminated with little actually having been produced. Lack of sales, contractual disagreements, and the interference of Anton Lorenz, who entered Breuer's business life once again in 1935, all played a part. The final blow to his hopes for the aluminum furniture was the diversion of metal production for military purposes in European countries preparing for the Second World War.[77]

Fig. 123. Flower tables, aluminum, 1932–33, shown on Wohnbedarf catalog page designed by Herbert Bayer. A variation on the B9 stool, these were also produced as a set of nesting tables with wooden tops.

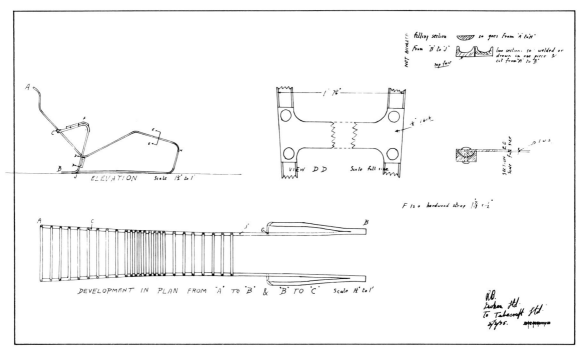

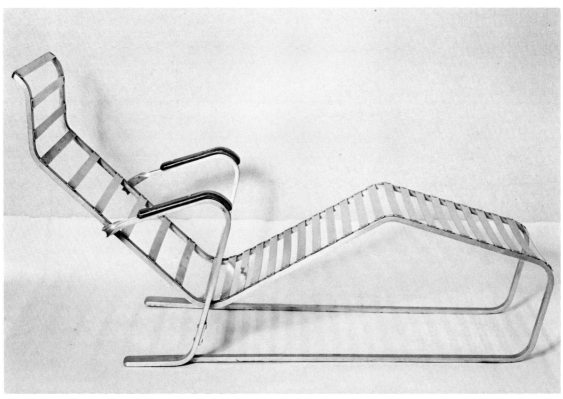

Fig. 124. Drawing of aluminum lounge chair, 1935. (Collection Pritchard Archive, University of Newcastle-upon-Tyne.) Drawn in England and sent to Tubecraft Ltd, who expressed interest in producing Breuer's design, this drawing demonstrated the shape of the chair before bending, the profile of the aluminum, and other details of construction.

Fig. 125. Frame for reclining chair, aluminum, steel, and wood. (Collection City of Bristol Museum and Art Gallery.) The flat bands of steel were used to support an upholstered cushion. This chair was originally owned by Crofton Gane and used in his Bristol home designed by Breuer.

England and Isokon
1935–37

During 1933 and 1934, Breuer divided his time between Zurich and Budapest, with occasional trips to Yugoslavia, Berlin, and Paris. He continued to travel wherever there was a chance for work. Walter Gropius, wanting to practice architecture as well as escape the increasingly oppressive political climate in Germany—where the Nazi-directed police had finally closed the Bauhaus in 1933—emigrated to England and formed a partnership with the British architect E. Maxwell Fry in October 1934. Gropius was also welcomed to England by Jack Pritchard, who, at the suggestion of P. Morton Shand, an architectural writer who had translated works by Gropius and Adolf Loos into English, attempted to find other sources of income for Gropius, including architectural commissions. Pritchard had met Gropius earlier and regarded him as "the leader of modern development in design."[78]

Little more than a month after Gropius arrived in England, Breuer was put into contact with F. S. R. Yorke, a British architect with modernist inclinations who also wrote extensively on modern architecture and was an editor of the *Architects' Journal*, a professional trade journal. Breuer envied the opportunities Gropius was to have for work, and wrote that he would willingly travel to England. He exhibited no particular urge to travel or move to England, as opposed to any other European country. The political circumstances that had led Gropius to leave Germany were not pressing for the young Hungarian then living in Central Europe. However, his somewhat itinerant life, and the uncertainty of his current project (the Doldertal flats), led him to think seriously of moving to England.

Yorke and Breuer began corresponding about the possibility of Breuer's coming to England to form a partnership with Yorke. Emigration to England was not possible without proof that one had savings as well as a steady income — partnership in a business greatly facilitated admission.

By April of 1935 Breuer was waiting for definite word from Yorke and, in expectation, was taking English lessons. During the summer of 1935 he visited England for at least one month, presumably to make final arrangements for his move. In October of 1935, one year after Gropius had arrived, Breuer moved to England.

Breuer was fully aware that his architectural partnership with Yorke would not provide sufficient income; like Gropius, he sought other possibilities for employment. He had corresponded for some time with Whitney Straight of Luminium Ltd about the possible production of his 1932 aluminum or tubular-steel furniture. But by August 1935, shortly before his arrival, negotiations had broken down.

Several proposed joint ventures between Pritchard and Gropius, mostly for modern housing developments, were never realized for a variety of reasons, including antagonism toward such novel buildings on the part of local authorities. Gropius and Pritchard had also been discussing plans for the formation of a furniture-producing branch of Isokon since early 1935. Gropius insisted that Breuer would have to be a part of any such venture in view of his extensive experience designing furniture; Pritchard readily agreed.

Fig. 126. Isokon long chair, laminated wood with upholstered cushion, 1935–36. (Collection The Museum of Modern Art, purchase.) By translating his aluminum chair into plywood, Breuer created a piece that was comparable to Aalto's plywood furniture. It was one of the earlier chairs of the 1930s that could be labeled "organic" or "biomorphic" in feeling.

ISOKON, FOR EASE, FOR EVER

Jack Pritchard is a unique individual who was the driving force behind several attempts at introducing modern architecture and design into England. Born in 1899 in London and educated in engineering and economics at Cambridge, Pritchard has a deep interest in design and design education, particularly as taught and practiced at the Bauhaus. After marrying his wife Molly, a bacteriologist, he went to work for the Venesta Plywood Company in 1925. He saw great potential for new uses of plywood and was responsible for Venesta's hiring Le Corbusier, Pierre Jeanneret, and Charlotte Perriand to execute a Venesta plywood exhibition stand in 1930 at the Building Trades Exhibition in London, as well as commissioning Moholy-Nagy to design magazine advertisements for Venesta. In 1930 and 1931 he traveled to see the Weissenhof housing settlement and the Bauhaus, making the latter trip with his friends Serge Chermayeff and Wells Coates, both of whom were strongly influenced by modernism. Pritchard was also quite active in the important Design and Industries Association and the new Modern Architectural Research group (MARS), the English chapter of the C.I.A.M.

Pritchard's most impressive accomplishment was his leading role in the founding of the Isokon Company, established in 1931 to promote and realize modern design. The term was a contraction of Isometric Unit Construction, and, as explained by Pritchard:

Isokon is a proprietary word that I have coined to denote the application of modern functional design to houses, flats, furniture and fittings. It also implies the idea of building in variety from standard units.[79]

In 1932, Isokon commissioned one of its cofounders, the architect Wells Coates, to design the first International Style apartment building in London, Lawn Road Flats, which was completed in 1934. At one time the home of Agatha Christie, Gropius, Breuer, and Moholy-Nagy, it was, at least for England, a radical modern building which in its overall design and the cooperative nature of its organization and daily life reflected the ideas of Pritchard and the principles of Isokon. It was against this background that Pritchard began talking to Gropius about the possibility of beginning a new company devoted to the manufacture of furniture.

The Isokon Furniture Company (fig. 127) was established at the end of November or beginning of December 1935. As Pritchard later explained:

The business was set up in order to exploit the growing demand for modern furniture. Our object was first to establish a good-will for authentic modern furniture in the high price market and secondly to develop from that position to the mass market.[80]

Following the original definition of Isokon, he set forth in more formal terms the policies of the new furniture company:

The general principle governing the policy will be in the designing, making and distributing of furniture, fittings, and equipment which will help to make contemporary living pleasanter, comfortable and more efficient.

Uniformity in character and design, combined with variety and individuality of each item, should be achieved.[81]

Pritchard's extensive experience with plywood, and his faith in it as a useful material,

---

Fig. 127. Logo of the Isokon Furniture Company, 1936.

hitherto largely unexploited, suggested from the very start that the new venture would concentrate on the production of plywood furniture. As explained in the memorandum cited above:

> The principal material to be used in the preliminary work must be plywood…
>
> Metal may be incorporated just where it performs a function better than plywood…
>
> The furniture will be primarily useful and its aesthetic qualities will be due to its form rather than superimposed ornament…
>
> In chairs, comfort will be the objective. Much recent modern furniture has failed to give the traditional English comfort tho' its form and shape has been pleasing…

The use of wood, therefore, warmer to the eye and touch, less austere than tubular steel, would be emphasized. And in the hopes of attracting a larger English market than had heretofore existed for modern furniture, com-

fort would be emphasized. The first Isokon chair discussed was therefore a comfortable reclining lounge chair, to be designed by Breuer, the idea for which came not from Breuer himself but from Gropius. At their first meeting, Gropius, with Pritchard's approval, suggested to Breuer that he design a plywood version of his aluminum lounge chair. The Isokon long chair, as it came to be known in the Isokon catalogs, was designed in December 1935, with work continuing on it into the first months of 1936.

THE RECLINING CHAIRS

Gropius' suggestion provided Breuer with the challenge of actually designing Isokon's first plywood reclining chair. His final design (fig. 126) closely followed the original aluminum

Fig. 128. Frame for Isokon short chair, laminated wood, 1936. The shorter length of the second lounge model exaggerated the curves in the design and made the chair seem even more organic than the Isokon long chair.

version (fig. 125), although he essayed several alternate models and numerous modifications took place during the first years of production.

Unlike the aluminum chair, the frame of the plywood chair could not practically be made from two continuous lengths of plywood; the plywood chair, in fact, required twice as many parts. Each side of the frame was composed of two separate pieces, since it was far more difficult and expensive to "split" a length of wood than a piece of aluminum. The outer piece, which formed part of the base and rose to become the arm and back support, was morticed and glued into the inner, longer length of wood, which served as the base of the chair and as the support for the lower part of the seat. As in the aluminum chair, a stabilizing crosspiece was added below the seat, joining each side of the frame. The seat was formed from a single piece of plywood morticed directly into the frame, in the middle of the back and just below the sitter's calf.

The plywood chair and its aluminum model differed in one basic respect, according to Breuer:

> …instead of building up a structure which is complete in itself so far as the load carrying members are concerned and then applying a seat to it, I now use frame members which only become a complete structure when parts of them are spanned by the seat.[82]

The frame of the aluminum chair was viewed as complete because each side of the frame was continuous and included the entire supporting frame of the back. In the wooden chair the frame stopped underneath the sitter's legs and did not continue to join the arms in any way; there was no structure for the back without the addition of the plywood seat and back. This lack of continuity, in Breuer's view, made the chair frame an incomplete, noncontinuous design.

The advantage of plywood construction was that the chair could be, and was, made under workshop conditions, whereas the aluminum chair required the relatively sophisticated facilities of a metal factory. Despite the use of a greater bulk of material in the plywood chair, it gave a similar resilience through less complicated construction.

The design of the Isokon short chair (fig. 128), as it was called, was nearly identical with that of the long chair. Different were the shape of the lower end of the seat and of the corresponding section of the frame. The seat curved downward at its bottom end, paralleling the shape of the frame — a necessary adjustment that took into account the posture of a person sitting in the shorter chair.

The first prototypes of the Isokon long chair were made by Harry Mansell, a furniture-maker who worked with Breuer, Gropius, and Pritchard in a tiny workshop, and later in a space next to the Lawn Road Flats. The frame pieces were made in the workshop, while the seats were ordered prebent from the Venesta factories in Estonia. Initially the frame was made by laminating thin veneers into pieces of the proper shape and size. They were bent and molded into shape in wooden forms made by Mansell. Because of the waste and expense of cutting the thin veneers, Pritchard began using veneers for the frames from the packing crates in which the seats were sent. Shortly thereafter they began collecting crates all over London to use for the seat frame. The seat, a half-inch plywood board, was formed at the Venesta factory immediately after the board had been glued, while it was still hot. It was then sent to London for assembly, and an upholstered cushion was applied, covering the entire seat.

After the first models were made, several problems presented themselves, and the design of the lounge chairs, especially the long chair, underwent a series of modifications. Breuer, unhappy with what he considered to be a lack of sufficient resilience in the seats, suggested making them not from conventional plywood (which is made from layers of veneer glued with the grain of adjoining plies at right angles), but from simple laminated veneers all glued with the grain running in the same direction. The result, thought Breuer, would be a more flexible seat. Pritchard, on the advice of Venesta, maintained that the seats would not be strong enough for normal use, and the material for the seat remained unchanged.

The most serious problem resulted from the attempted translation of the aluminum chair into plywood. Whereas the aluminum chair could deflect from side to side with little or no adverse effect to the structural integrity of the frame or arms, in the wooden chair this freedom of lateral movement led to the loosening of the mortice-and-tenon joint of the seat and arm, and to the weakening of the laminates of the arm itself, into which the seat was fitted.

Breuer attempted to overcome this weakness by strengthening the arm, placing a perpendicular strip of wood under it. This strip, or fin, added in early 1936, gave the arm a T-shaped section and provided additional support to the main load-bearing element of the design. The first Isokon lounge chairs sold commercially, as well as all those later produced, contained the fin; other modifications were introduced when it proved insufficient to solve the entire problem.

In the first versions of the chair, the seat was attached to the frame by a mortice-and-tenon joint. The seat board was cut with two plywood "ears" protruding from each side of the seat. These ears were fitted and glued into the frame below the sitter's calf and behind the back. In some early versions of the chair the laminates of the plywood seat had begun to come apart or were cracking around the area of the ear. In a second version of 1936, the ears were reinforced by the addition of an extra layer of veneer around the area of each ear. Despite these changes, some examples of

the chair still lacked sufficient strength at this critical point.

During the 1950s and '60s, Pritchard continued working on the chair, with Breuer's assistance via transatlantic correspondence. The ears were dispensed with and the seat was attached by means of two horizontal members spanning the entire width of the seat. These lateral members were inserted into each side of the frame just as the ears had been; the seat was placed on top of them. The cross members thus carried the weight formerly carried only by the seat. This finally solved the problem.

Other subsequent modifications included the alteration of the pitch of the seat. The shape of the seat, and therefore the size of the supporting frame, also underwent several changes. The proportions of the chair were gradually changed, as were several details, most notably the "split" articulation of the base. The original version had clearly expressed the different construction of the plywood chair as opposed to its aluminum model: that the base and frame were made from two entirely separate lengths of wood, not from a single piece split in half. In later versions there was no attempt to articulate the rear of the base as two separate pieces; rather, they were made to appear as one piece. Finally, the gentle rise in the long outer base piece, a feature found in Breuer's tubular-steel and aluminum furniture and designed to add even more resilience to the frame, was turned into a pronounced hump.

These modifications of the chair, added as "improvements," resulted in what was undoubtedly a more structurally sound design, but also diminished the visual impact of the original. The problem posed was, and is, a significant one for designers and producers: how could one reconcile the original, aesthetically more satisfactory solutions with the later, less-interesting models, which benefited from the experience of years of use?

Breuer designed at least ten variants of the Isokon lounge chairs, none of which were put into production, but all of which he patented (figs. 129, 130). In all of these designs the principal idea remained the same: a plywood frame made of cantilevered elements that would provide a resilient structure onto which the seat would be applied. In all of the designs resilience was sought not only through the design of the frame or of the seat, but through maximizing the possibilities for spring in both. In none of the chairs was the design of the frame continuous.

OTHER ISOKON FURNITURE DESIGNS

In February of 1936, Breuer designed a set of plywood nesting tables (fig. 131) that were also based on an earlier design: ten tubular-steel nesting stools designed at the Bauhaus in 1925–26. Their translation into wood a decade later reflected not the exact design of the original, but rather the overall conception applied to a completely different material. The new design for plywood allowed an advance over the original model, since the table could now be cut and bent from a single piece of ply-

wood. It was as economical and compact as a nesting-table design could be. The same material was used as that employed for the seats of the lounge chair. At first, both were made in Estonia by Venesta for Isokon, and both required only a simple one-step molding process. They were later manufactured in England.

The shape of the tables, especially the side and legs, represented something completely new in Breuer's design. Although a structural rationale can be found for the shape, the tables nonetheless partook of a freer sense of form, characterized by curved and animated shapes, which would become more common in furniture, especially plywood furniture, of the 1940s. (The freedom of the cutout-plywood shape began to interest Breuer increasingly at this time.)

In order to assure the stability and structural integrity of the small, thin tables, a wide expanse of wood was necessary at the top of each side. As the legs descended from the table top, less support became necessary as long as the legs were sufficiently stabilized against possible lateral movement at the top. Eventually Breuer designed the table with added bracing between the legs. Although this design was patented it was never produced, since the

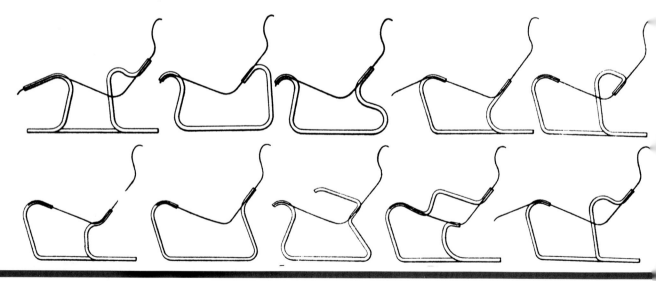

Fig. 129. Patent drawings for variations on Isokon lounge chairs, applied for 10 July 1936.

extra work and material meant that the low cost of the table could not be maintained.

The nesting-table design was enlarged for a dining table that Breuer designed around the same time and also patented during the summer of 1936.[83] This design, as eventually produced, was altered by the five-piece construction of the table, necessary because the table was too large to make from a single piece of plywood. The top was made from a single piece that overlapped the four legs, each one of which was reinforced by a vertical fin that ran at a perpendicular the entire length of the leg. Another variant of the table design (fig. 132), not put into production, had a series of overlapping supports that appeared to be made from smaller sizes of the table nested within, and attached to, the underside of the table, thereby connecting and supporting the top and the legs.

Breuer designed several versions of an Isokon stacking chair. In the design of seat and legs, the first model (fig. 133) closely resembled the nesting table. Continuous with the seat was a back support, or brace, to which was attached a small back with a curved top for easy handling. The idea of a chair made from only two pieces of wood, lightweight and stackable, and of modern design, seemed perfect for the marketplace. Pritchard thought it would be Isokon's most successful model. But the back brace was not strong enough to support the back, and the chair suffered also from an overall lack of stability. An armchair version of the stacking chair, also designed in 1936 and known only in drawings, was plagued with similar problems.

Breuer and Pritchard thought they could solve the problems in the chair's designs first by stretching braces between the front and back legs underneath the seat; although this was successful, the number of chairs that could be stacked in a pile was reduced. Second, they sought to prevent the back from breaking by making the back from a separate piece of plywood, attached to the underside of the seat. Although this solution was not successful and the first version of the chair was abandoned, it did provide an idea for the final solution for an Isokon stacking chair.

The stacking chair that was finally manufactured and sold by Isokon (figs. 134, 135) was a far more complex but only slightly less problematic design. It dated from late 1936. Less homogeneous in design, it lacked the structural and visual continuity characteristic of Breuer's chairs. Nine pieces were required for the construction of each stacking side chair. Two pairs of legs were spanned by wide plywood braces running from front leg to rear. The four legs and braces were covered with an extraordinarily thin plywood seat, which was intended to add resilience to the chair.

Attached to the rear legs and back of the seat, and passing through the seat at the rear, was the back brace (fig. 134), to which was screwed the same back used in the first design. Making the chair from so many parts and dispensing with the careful bends required in the first design eliminated the problem of weak areas of plywood. Everyone professed satisfaction with the chair, and it was put into

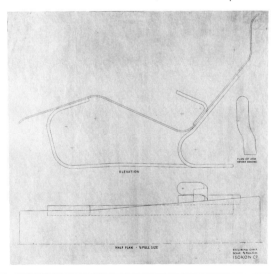

Fig. 130. Drawing, alternate design for Isokon long chair, ink on oilcloth, 1936. (Collection Victoria and Albert Museum, London.) The arms were bent from separate pieces of wood and then attached to the seat and frame.

133

Fig. 131. Isokon nesting tables, plywood, 1936. (Collection The Museum of Modern Art, purchase.) The tables were cut and bent from a single board and originally manufactured in Estonia by Venesta for Isokon. They were testimony to Breuer's desire to adapt his favorite design (the tubular-steel stool) to every possible material.

Fig. 132. Alternate version of the Isokon dining table, plywood, 1936. The original version of the table weighed only twenty-one pounds and was stabilized by the use of a brace which stretched from top to bottom of each two-piece leg. The alternate version, illustrated above, an example of which was used for the Ventris apartment, substituted a series of overlapping braces.

production. Yet it too suffered from an overall lack of stability. It had no inherent strength; everything was dependent on glued or bolted joints—of which there were too many.

This final version of the Isokon stacking chair was never designed as an armchair, for the complexity of the design made the addition of an arm virtually impossible. Breuer's desire to design a new stacking armchair led him to work on a new aluminum model, but no photos or drawings of that chair survive, and recollections vary as to its appearance.

Although Isokon did manage to stay in business for a few years, producing a modest number of designs by Breuer, Gropius, Harry Mansell, Egon Riss, Wells Coates, and Jack Pritchard, it constantly had to face the kinds of difficulties often encountered in new ventures. The fact that certain parts and certain models were made in Estonia led to problems of long-distance communication. Unforeseeable delays and mistakes had both parties at wit's end on more than one occasion. Experimentation with molded-plywood furniture was relatively recent. And although there was the example of Aalto in Finland (fig. 137)—he had been designing successful molded-plywood furniture since 1931—most of the "bugs" in Isokon's designs could not be ironed out of the production process; for example, problems were found with glues unable to withstand heat and humidity. The taste of the English public was another problem. And even though Pritchard was pleased with the rate of three to six Isokon long chairs produced per week in 1938, the output was insufficient to guarantee a secure future for Isokon. Finally, inevitably, there was the coming of the Second World War, which completely destroyed Isokon's chance for large-scale success.

Despite the fact that Breuer's Isokon long chair especially has always been held in high esteem, it has never sold in large quantity. And despite Pritchard's attempts to revive Isokon,

the firm never prospered. Yet the Isokon venture was one of the highlights of the brief life of early modernism in England, and Breuer's long chair influenced many furniture designers and manufacturers in the years to come.

HEAL'S SEVEN ARCHITECTS EXHIBITION, 1936

At the same time that Breuer continued to work on the Isokon chairs, he undertook a number of different projects for both furniture and architectural design. In 1936 he was commissioned by Heal & Son, the venerable London firm of furniture dealers, to provide designs for an exhibition of furniture by seven architects. The exhibition was arranged by Gropius' partner, Maxwell Fry. Breuer's space was devoted to a living room (fig. 136) with a finely detailed wall unit, "metal plastic" wall paneling, and a bent-sycamore lounge chair.

Fig. 133. Isokon side chair, plywood, 1936. The original version of the Isokon stacking chair was based on Breuer's nesting-table design.

The Breuer wall unit, which also was executed in light sycamore, was typical except for one feature: three of the units on the right side had fall fronts that were counterbalanced by tubular-steel extensions filled with lead shot, the purpose of which was to balance the closed doors, to which could be attached heavy objects such as a typewriter or record player. These hinged fronts were faced with black glass.

The lounge chair was an unusually free and decorative design formed from two continuous lengths of bent and molded sycamore laminates, with a crosspiece between them, under the seat. The wood-framed tufted upholstered seat and back were attached to the frame in three separate pieces. The design showed the increasing influence of Aalto's masterful bent plywood chairs on Breuer's work; but instead of choosing the type of cantilevered design used by Aalto (fig. 137), Breuer elected to have the rear of his base rise up to carry the rear of the seat—hence the

continuation of the curve.[84] The result was an oddly styled chair with free-form, flowing sides. It was a design that Breuer later removed from retrospective surveys of his work.

Breuer designed another chair for Heal's, a reclining chair (fig. 138) made from both molded and cutout plywood parts. The chair was a bulky construction that showed the direction toward which Breuer's furniture designs were tending: toward free-form cutout-plywood constructions that seemed to have little to do with his earlier furniture. The overstuffed lounge or reclining chair was, so Breuer was learning, the easiest furniture type to sell, at least to English producers. Heal's apparently sold a modest number of Breuer's chairs, at least for two years, for Breuer was paid royalties in 1937 and 1938. As Heal's was becoming increasingly known for selling a good selection of modern furniture, including items by Isokon and Serge Chermayeff among others, Walter Gropius attempted to convince the firm to hire a number of modernists to design furniture and also to serve as advisors, but the plan was rejected.

BREUER & YORKE, ARCHITECTURAL COMMISSIONS

Breuer's admission to England was predicated on his assertions to the Home Office in August 1935 that he would soon be entering into an architectural partnership with F. S. R. Yorke. He had visited England that summer, and although their formal agreement was not reached until November, Breuer had already designed one interior which, like all of his English architectural work, was published under the name of Breuer & Yorke.

This first commission, carried out during mid-1935, before Breuer had taken up residence in England, was the renovation of a nondescript free-standing two-story house

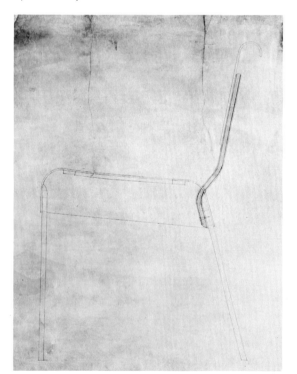

Fig. 134. Drawing of the final version of the Isokon stacking chair, 1936. The drawing clearly shows the multipart construction of the chair and demonstrates the inherent weakness of the frame.

recently purchased by Crofton Gane of Bristol. Gane, the Director of P. E. Gane Ltd, a leading manufacturer and distributor of reproduction and modern furniture, was actively involved in attempts to promote modern design in England. As a member of the Design and Industries Association, and through his own work as a furniture producer manufacturing modern furniture and selling items produced by Isokon, Artek (Aalto furniture), and Best & Company (modern British lighting), Gane became one of the most important champions of modern design in the English marketplace. In addition to hiring Breuer to renovate his house, he retained him as a "consultant designer" to the firm and assisted him in obtaining other commissions.

Gane desired a house that would be "neither a minimum nor a luxury dwelling, but (internally at least) a comfortable and elegant modern home."[85] The new rooms were to serve as "'show' rooms" of well-designed and -crafted modern furnishings, including products of P. E. Gane, which either sold or manufactured all of the furniture in the house.

Because of a limited budget of fourteen hundred pounds, the project involved mainly interior renovation. The project, according to Breuer, represented

> an effort to incorporate modern ideas and contemporary requirements without considerable structural changes. This meant mainly reconstruction inside with corresponding changes in the equipment.[86]

Breuer's renovation did include a limited amount of alteration to the exterior of the house, mainly changes in the size and shape of windows and doorways. On the other hand, the changes in the interior were substantial. The Gane commission resulted in one of the most striking new interiors in England, and a significant work in Breuer's career.

The main internal alterations were the in-

Fig. 135. Isokon side chairs, plywood, 1936–37. (Collection The Museum of Modern Art, gift of Eliot Noyes.) The production version of the chair was made from too many pieces of plywood; the original intent of the design was lost and the result was less than graceful.

stallation of a new, modern staircase and landing; replacement of the plumbing and electrical systems and the installation of an electric heating system; the opening of the dining-room wall onto the garden; and the installation of a wall or corrugated-asbestos paneling in the dining room.

The entrance to the house was dominated by a staircase, a light and transparent structure made with tubular-steel balustrade, metal supports, and risers all painted gray and blue. Beyond the staircase, its former wall removed, was a garden-study (fig. 139), which was furnished with a built-in sycamore desk and bookcase unit placed against a white wall. On the opposite, blue wall was a tubular-

Fig. 136. Living room for Heal's 7 Architects Exhibition, 1936. Through the many published projects and exhibitions he designed while briefly in England, Breuer's work became widely known.

Fig. 137. Alvar Aalto, armchair, bent plywood with upholstery, manufactured by Artek, Finland, c. 1933. Aalto's first chair designs were said to have been inspired by Breuer's Bauhaus tubular-steel furniture; during the 1930s Aalto's bent-plywood chairs had a strong effect on Breuer and virtually all designers working in wood.

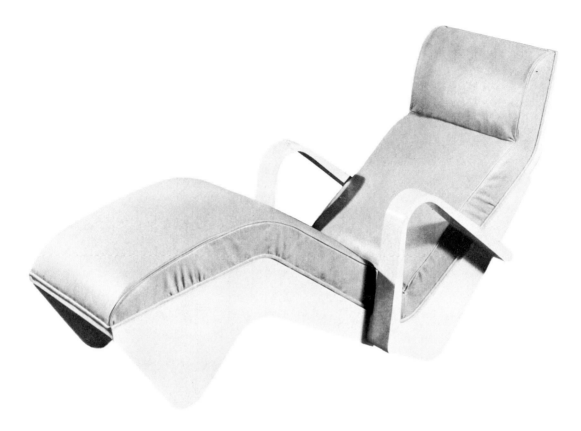

steel and glass pier table with a semicircular top, beneath which was an electric heater. Plain gray carpeting covered the floor, and cream-colored curtains hung at the windows. The room was further opened to light by the enlargement of the windows over the desk and by the glass doors that opened onto the garden. Breuer's aluminum chairs were used throughout.

The adjacent dining room (fig. 140), one end of which also opened onto the garden, was a strikingly dramatic room owing to the sparseness of the furnishing and the undulating white asbestos wall. The wall, which had a heater placed in its middle, functioned as a powerful decorative element and was left bare

except for a low black sideboard with glass doors placed against it. The opposite wall, also painted white, was hung with a long horizontal band of black-lacquered wall cabinets, some with drop-down wooden fronts, others with clear sliding glass fronts. The aluminum side chairs were upholstered in ''porcelain-blue fabric stitched with lines of raised white thread.''[87] The table was black-lacquered birch with legs to match. The floor was covered with Indian-red carpeting.

The first-floor drawing room (fig. 141) had light maple paneling on the walls and gray carpeting on the floor. Here the ceiling was white with a slight bluish tint. The entire room was oriented around the only working fire-

Fig. 138. Reclining chair, plywood with upholstery, 1936. Designed for Heal's and later reworked for the 1938 Frank house. Although not Breuer's most memorable design, it anticipated by several years Frederick Kiesler's highly regarded free-form seating/display units for Peggy Guggenheim's Art of This Century gallery.

place in the house, although in one corner a desk, table, and bookcase were grouped to provide a study area. The room was furnished with specially designed light-maple and sycamore furniture, including two Aaltoesque armchairs. Lighting throughout the house was handled by Breuer's favorite reflecting lamps, supplemented by desk or reading lights added where needed. As usual, Breuer used no standing lamps.

Upstairs there were three bedrooms and a study-bedroom. All, including the master bedroom, contained bent-plywood beds (fig. 142) of light brown grained maple which were based on Breuer's tubular-steel beds. They were simple, geometrical constructions, with identical soft-edged rectangles for headboard and footboard, reminiscent of the side pieces of Breuer's wooden Harnishmacher chair (fig. 108). The beds, although much admired at the time, were never offered commercially. They were covered with dark brown camel's-hair

bedspreads. The master bedroom also contained an adjustable dressing mirror and table, a familiar Breuer design, which was fitted with a built-in light at the base of the mirror and a black glass top for the brown maple drawers. Against one bedroom wall stood a large sycamore wardrobe with sliding doors. The master-bedroom floors were covered with light brown cork, a new element in a Breuer interior. The overall brownish tone of the room was complemented by dark brown window drapes. Aluminum furniture was used in all of the bedrooms, and the Wohnbedarf Breuer desk (fig. 114) was used in the study-bedroom.

The design of the Gane house was a highlight of Breuer's English period. The style was softer than that of his early designs, more adapted to English tastes. The result was a freer and more relaxed interior which, nonetheless, was harmonious and impeccably detailed.

Possibly before his own house was com-

Fig. 139. Garden room, Gane house, Bristol, 1935. Photograph taken from garden side of room, looking toward the entrance hallway with tubular-steel staircase. The semicircular steel-and-glass pier table was a design Breuer had used in the study of the 1930 Paris exhibition and would later repeat in the Ventris apartment and Frank house.

Fig. 140. Dining room, Gane house, Bristol, 1935. The undulating asbestos wall created an unusually dynamic spatial effect in the room.

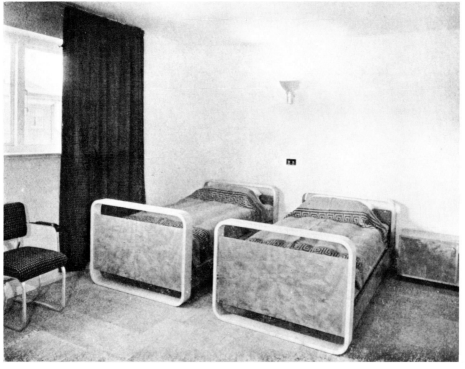

Fig. 141. Living room, Gane house, Bristol, 1935. The room contained a large number of specially designed wooden pieces, including the Aalto-inspired armchair.

Fig. 142. Bedroom, Gane house, Bristol, 1935. The beds were direct translations of Breuer's earlier tubular-steel beds into bent plywood.

plete, Gane commissioned Breuer to design his firm's exhibition pavilion for the July 1936 Royal Agricultural Show in Bristol (figs. 143–45). The pavilion was a marked departure from Breuer's earlier work and gave him the opportunity to demonstrate his talents to a wide audience, especially through its extensive publication. The pavilion was designed solely for the display of Gane's furniture, and although perceived by much of the public as a house, it did not conform to the usual domestic requirements, since it lacked a kitchen and sanitary facilities.

The open planning of the pavilion and the details of construction were completely Miesian in origin. The structure was made of local Cotswold stone on concrete footings with roof and structural supports of wood. Large plate-glass windows, some sliding, opened up the interior to the outside. Birch plywood was used on the interior of some of the rough stone walls and also for flooring.

The interior of the house (fig. 144) was an exercise in open and flexible planning. The architectural impact of flat plywood-covered walls and the wide and open plate-glass windows at times threatened to overwhelm the

purpose of the pavilion, which was the display of furniture. Much of the plywood flooring was covered with simple rugs to allow the wooden furniture to be seen against a background of a different material. The sense of freedom of the pavilion and of the interior came not only from the overall openness of the house, but also from such details as the gentle curve of the living-room wall, a feature seldom seen at this time in domestic interiors. The overall success of the building relied heavily on the contrasts of light and dark, smooth and rough, transparent and solid materials.

Of singular importance in Breuer's work was his use of the local stone, which was handled in the traditional squared-rubble fashion. His willingness to introduce regional materials and construction techniques served to bring the new and startling modernist aesthetic somewhat closer to the local population. This remained the case when Breuer moved to the United States and absorbed the vernacular forms of New England architecture. It would, however, be a mistake to see Breuer's handling of stone and the use of the curved interior wall as completely original ideas; they derived from Le Corbusier's Pavillon Suisse (1930–32) in Paris, which Breuer must have known well. In fact, the steady integration of masonry into Breuer's work during the next several decades owed a great deal to Le Corbusier, more, perhaps, than Breuer would ever acknowledge.

Breuer also undertook the installation of a London apartment for Mrs. Ventris and her young son in 1936. The apartment was in a new, modern apartment building referred to as Highpoint, in Highgate, designed by Berthold Lubetkin and his Tecton group in 1935. Lubetkin was a Russian-born architect who had emigrated to England, where his firm not only constructed an unusually large number of International Style buildings, but also served as a

Fig. 143. Breuer & Yorke, plan, Gane Pavilion, Royal Agricultural Show, Bristol, 1936.

training ground for young English architects.

The rectangular apartment (fig. 146) contained seven rooms. Upon entering one walked past the kitchen and dining room and entered the large living room (fig. 147) with corner study. On one wall of the living room was a wide expanse of windows. The opposite wall was covered with grass matting, a material favored by Breuer at this time. Behind the couch, at a right angle to this wall, was a translucent screen of the same matting, which masked a narrow entrance into the private areas of the apartment. The room was also furnished with an Isokon long chair and nesting stools. In the center of the room was a free-standing electric heater. Freed of the necessity

Fig. 144. Breuer & Yorke, interior, Gane Pavilion, Royal Agricultural Show, Bristol, 1936. The open planning, the attempt to merge or at least bring together interior and exterior, the use of rough masonry with glass and plywood, would all become typical of Breuer's work.

Fig. 145. Breuer & Yorke, Gane Pavilion, Royal Agricultural Show, Bristol, 1936. Although largely based on the ideas of Mies for its plan and on Le Corbusier for the extensive use of rough masonry and a curved interior wall, the Gane Pavilion suggested the direction Breuer's work would take during the coming years.

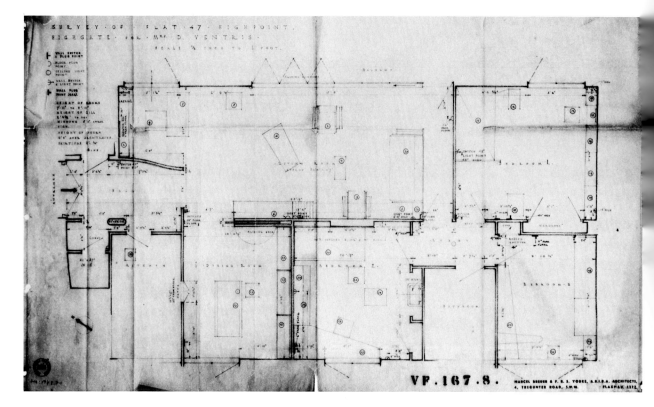

to use a fireplace located below a flue, Breuer chose to use the heater as a "social focus" of the room. (Although the idea was intriguing, what the room as designed by Breuer precisely lacked was a central focus.) Among the items of specially designed furniture were a polished sycamore gramophone cabinet hung from the wall but also supported by two tubular-steel legs, and a pair of cocktail cupboards, also in sycamore, with polished blue interiors; one of these was hung in the corner, rising to the top of the walls, while the other sat on the floor. Attached to the side of the upper one was an adjustable table lamp. Most of the lighting in the house consisted of reflectors attached to the upper wall.

Although Breuer had always attempted, through the use of tubular-steel furniture and of wall units lifted above the interior floors, to open up the interior space as much as possi-

ble, the heavy upholstered furniture he designed for the apartment suggested a new view of the possibilities of design for interior spaces. In particular, he designed a cutout-plywood chair and couch (figs. 147, 148) for Mrs. Ventris with eccentric, organic forms that prefigure much of the furniture he would design in America between 1938 and 1940. They became massive architectural elements that served to define the space of the room while also making it less open or flexible.

The Ventris dining room (fig. 149) was the usual but completely successful combination of elements, which in the Ventris apartment included an Isokon table design in black laminated wood. The floors of the dining and living rooms were covered with white woolen pile carpet.

The bedrooms were fitted with built-in furniture: desks, bookcases, and cabinets in the

Fig. 146. Breuer & Yorke, plan, Ventris apartment, London, 1936. (Collection Royal Institute of British Architects.)

boy's room and a more unusual storage system in the master bedroom (fig. 150), where a low group of dressers and cabinets hanging from the wall was broken up by a thin vertical dressing mirror, flanked by round adjustable viewing mirrors. It was a strong sculptural composition. Equally interesting was the series of drawers on both sides of the mirrors which pivoted on hinges. They added a new element to Breuer's cabinetwork, one on which he would attempt variations in later years.

In March 1937, Walter Gropius left England to immigrate to the United States, where he was to be appointed professor of architecture at Harvard University. Gropius had been disappointed at the few building commissions he had obtained in England and, like so many other European émigrés, looked to the United States as a country full of opportunity. Breuer began to think of leaving also. It seems likely

Fig. 147. Breuer & Yorke, living room, Ventris apartment, London, 1936.

Fig. 148. Armchair, Ventris apartment, London, 1936. The freely cutout sides of the chair provided the basis for Breuer's later free-form chairs and couches.

145

that Gropius told Breuer that he would try to obtain a teaching position for him.

During the summer of 1937 Breuer sailed to the United States, ostensibly to visit Gropius, but also to investigate the possibilities for American production of his Isokon and Embru aluminum furniture. Before he left, Yorke warned him that he would probably not be returning. Yorke was right. In the fall of 1937 Breuer received an appointment to teach architecture at Harvard. He returned to England briefly at the end of the year to wrap up his business affairs.

Breuer left England after less than two full years of residence. Isokon continued, although still struggling. Attempts had been made to interest a number of English manufacturers, including Pel, Cox, Duncan Miller, Metal Furniture Works Ltd, London Aluminium Co., and Luminium Ltd, in producing Breuer's tubular-

steel or aluminum furniture. His designs were eventually rejected by all. Schemes to design furniture, or act as an advisor for Heal & Son and Simpson Ltd, were short-lived. But compared to many architects, Breuer designed and built a surprising amount in England.

He designed what might be called the most important example of modernist furniture in England: the Isokon long chair. He designed one of the finest interiors of the period: the Gane house. And he also designed one of the most interesting and successful modern buildings in England: the Gane Pavilion at the Royal Agricultural Fair. At a time when most British designers ignored what Breuer called the New Architecture, and when only a handful seemed to have an ability to work comfortably within the new modernist mode, it was Breuer who provided many of the best examples of modern design work in England.

Fig. 149. Breuer & Yorke, dining room, Ventris apartment, London, 1936. The dining table was similar to the model shown in fig. 132.

Fig. 150. Breuer & Yorke, bedroom, Ventris apartment, London, 1936. Breuer's designs for dressing mirrors and tables or cabinets were always accomplished; those in the Ventris apartment were particularly successful.

The United States
1937–67

In the fall of 1937, Breuer moved to Cambridge, Massachusetts, where he would live and work for nearly a decade. Gropius and Breuer's first American houses, which were widely published, had a profound effect on American domestic architecture. As teachers they influenced an entire generation of architects—many of them among the more well known and established of current American architects—and were responsible for bringing to the U.S. architectural ideas and principles which have only recently come under criticism.

Their earliest American buildings (figs. 151–54) showed the openness with which they looked at the traditional architecture of New England and the vitality with which they adapted its various forms and materials. These houses tended to be designed with simple and undogmatic geometrical plans and were characterized by the use of rough stone and clapboard or siding and, in interiors, warm plywood walls, glass brick, and built-in cabinetwork in white or natural-colored woods. The brick and stucco of Europe were replaced by the wood and stone of America. In the best of the New England houses, designed between 1938 and 1941, the combining of the modernist idiom with local materials, and the expansion of the formal vocabulary to include less rigidly geometrical, curved forms, resulted in new solutions for American domestic architecture

that were much imitated even into the 1950s.

Much of the credit for developing this new American version of a modern architecture must go to Breuer. For although the Gropius-Breuer partnership was a true collaboration, it was often the ideas and hand of the younger Breuer that determined the ultimate appearance and detailing of the buildings.

While Gropius and Breuer built houses together and taught at Harvard, Breuer also continued to design furniture. His furniture projects were mostly confined to the years 1938–42, 1944–45, and 1948–49. Most of the designs, some of which were actually redesigns, were for various types of cutout-plywood furniture. Although Breuer had designed plywood furniture for years, his concentration on the material in the United States was related to contemporary American taste, which much preferred the warmth of wood to the shine of metal. Metal furniture was produced in large quantity in the United States, but its use was largely confined to offices, restaurants, and domestic kitchens. For the most part, it was still not considered appropriate for use in the home. The use of plywood furniture, and of natural-finished wood, on the other hand, became widespread in American interiors of this period, and reflected the broadening influence of Aalto and other Scandinavian designers.

BRYN MAWR DORMITORY FURNITURE

When Bryn Mawr College began building a new Gothic dormitory in 1937, the James E. Rhoads Residence Hall, it was decided that the furniture would be modern.[88] The idea of holding a competition for the dormitory furniture was discussed, but was abandoned because of the lack of time and funds required for such an undertaking. After an unsuccessful search for appropriate furniture in stores in New York and Philadelphia, it was decided to

Fig. 151. Gropius and Breuer, entrance, Gropius house, Lincoln, Mass., 1938. In the Gropius house, the delicate handling of the vertical wood paneling and glass bricks was one of the many indications of Breuer's unique talent for careful detailing in his buildings. The lamp had been made in the Bauhaus metal workshop.

Fig. 152. Gropius and Breuer, staircase, Haggerty house, Cohasset, Mass., 1938. A particularly fine example of Breuer's dynamic treatment of staircases, it had many imitators during the 1940s.

Fig. 153. Gropius and Breuer, Breuer house, Lincoln, 1939. View from the living room looking down to the dining room and up to the second-floor hall and bedroom. Breuer's first house for himself (built as a small "bachelor's residence") was dominated by the warm tones of redwood, grass matting, and stone, all within a spatially complex yet eminently satisfying design.

send a set of general specifications to Breuer at Harvard and request designs. The specifications for a dormitory-room set of desk and chair, dresser, mirror, and bookshelves were sent to Breuer at the end of 1937 or beginning of 1938. The designs he offered were accepted, and work on prototypes was begun shortly thereafter at Harvard. By March 1938, models of the furniture were sent to the College and were returned for minor modification. And by October of 1938, when the dormitory was officially opened, the new furniture (fig. 155) was in place. It was greeted with praise by College and alumnae press.

The Bryn Mawr desk chair was made from cutout-plywood sides, a solid wood seat and back, and thick wooden dowel supports stretched between the sides of the frame. Each side of the frame was made from two pieces of cutout plywood. The front legs and main part of the seat frame on each side were made from a single L-shaped piece of plywood; the rear legs and back frame were designed as a long upright that bulged out at the center, providing a wider area of contact between the two pieces. In the first version of the chair, both the seat and back were made from a series of thick dowels covered with what appears in surviving photographs to be upholstery. In the final version, the seat and back were made from solid wood, while two dowels were left exposed behind the seat where the

Fig. 154. Gropius and Breuer, Chamberlain cottage, Weyland, Mass., 1940. The cottage was widely published when it was built. The interior demonstrated the successful combination of the materials favored by Breuer at this time and offered a particularly fine example of his use of the fireplace as a space divider and sculptural object.

two pieces of each side of the frame were joined, and just below the front of the seat—both critical stress points.

In addition to the Bryn Mawr chair, Breuer provided a desk which in overall design closely resembled many of the built-in and free-standing desks that he had designed during the preceding fifteen years. The drawer unit and bent-plywood leg were joined by an ample tabletop and additional cross-bracing. Virtually the same top was used on the four-drawer dresser, a simple and functional design with overhanging top and with drawer pulls cut into each drawer. The set was completed with a plain rectangular mirror attached to a high wall molding with long metal strips, and a two-shelf bookshelf hung above the desk. All of the dormitory furniture was executed in maple or birch in a light, golden-yellow natural lacquered finish.

The furniture was straightforward and un-affected, eminently suited for heavy use in a college dormitory. The chair and desk represented a further development of previous cutout-plywood designs, and the commission gave Breuer the opportunity to adapt these designs for mass production.

FRANK HOUSE

In 1939, Gropius and Breuer were commissioned to design a house for the Frank family of Pittsburgh. At the time, it was described as "probably the largest residence ever built in the International Style."[89] The clients were socially prominent citizens of Pittsburgh who had built their house in the fashionable community of Oakland. They had few furnishings that they wished the new house to accommodate, but they wanted a large house, the size of which grew several times during the planning stages. Because of the extensive program required by the clients, and the fact that all of

the interior furnishings and fittings were designed by the architects, the house represented one of the most complete interiors ever designed by Breuer. For although Breuer and Gropius collaborated on the plans for the house, it was Breuer who was responsible for most of the interior work, including the furniture. Virtually all the objects in the house—chairs and tables, wall units, and lighting fixtures, even a small radio and piano—were specially designed for the commission.

The clients required six bedrooms, three studies or dens, three dressing rooms, two spacious halls used as sitting rooms, a living and dining room, nine bathrooms, two bars, a kitchen, an indoor heated swimming pool, a game room, elevator, two servant's rooms, garage, terraces, and at least nine other subsidiary rooms for laundry, storage, and mechanical services. The resulting four-story house was steel-framed and faced with brick and local fieldstone.

Visitors entered the house through a ground-floor entrance (fig. 156), the walls of which were made of glass brick. Against one wall was a table with a base of glass bricks

Fig. 155. Dormitory furniture, Rhoads Hall, Bryn Mawr College, 1938. Breuer's first furniture commission in the United States was based on his earlier experiments with cutout-plywood furniture in England. Each furniture group consisted of a desk, chair, dresser, bookshelf, and mirror.

supporting a glass top (fig. 184). This was perhaps the earliest example of Breuer's monumental or architectural furniture, which would become more common during the 1950s. The hall led directly to a staircase ascending to the first floor, where most of the public rooms were located.

At the top of the staircase was a reception hall (fig. 157) with walls of travertine and English harewood ply paneling. Several pieces of furniture, including a long curved sofa, were executed in pear wood. A small rectangular table, placed between chairs, was designed with lucite legs.

The adjacent dining room (fig. 158) used the same materials for the furniture, walls, and floors as the hall. At one end, easily set apart by a pair of folding screens, was a dining alcove, presumably for the children. Small shelves and ceiling reflectors were attached to the wall. A pinkish oatmeal colored upholstery covered the cantilevered dining chairs, a new version of Breuer's cutout-plywood furniture. The entire house was dominated by the tones of brown carpeting and upholstery and by the natural light color of

the wood paneling and furniture. The travertine walls in many of the first-floor rooms were also light in tone.

The long, narrow living room was oriented to the fireplace, set into a curved wall of travertine. Brown and red upholsteries covered the extremely long curved couch and chairs which stretched from one end of the room to the other. The design of this living-room furniture seemed typical of 1940s American upholstered furniture: soft-edges, bulky cushions, a certain lack of definition in the shapes. Draperies, which were used in abundance throughout the house, could be drawn across all of the windows. No doors were used between living room and the adjacent rooms.

Beyond the living room lay the main study (fig. 159), which was fitted with a wall of bookshelves and a master control panel for heat, air conditioning, music, etc. Its walls were paneled in pear wood and the same local fieldstone that covered the exterior of the house. All of the furniture here was made of pear wood also. An armchair similar in design to those in the dining room faced a plywood

desk. Other furniture included a lounge chair based on Breuer's original Heal's design (fig. 138) and a shorter armchair of bulky proportions. A wide couch was placed before the bookcase, and a simple table with an X-shaped base and round top was used here as in other rooms of the house. The study looked onto an indoor terrarium.

The upstairs rooms included many built-in desks, tables, and bookshelves. An odd side chair with an X-shaped base (fig. 161) was used at most of the desks or dressing tables, which were made of either redwood, English harewood, or maple plywoods. A set of rectilinear upholstered furniture surrounded the fireplace in the upstairs hall (fig. 162). Hooked brown-taupe carpets covered most of the

Fig. 157. Staircase and first-floor landing, Frank house, Pittsburgh, 1939. View from the dining room. Both the staircase and couch were emphatically curved to echo the exterior of the house.

Fig. 158. Gropius and Breuer, dining room, Frank house, Pittsburgh, 1939. Breuer designed the furniture, including the dining tables with lucite legs and the unusual cantilevered side chairs and armchairs, as well as the lighting, most of which consisted of metal wall fixtures providing indirect lighting.

153

Fig. 159. First-floor study, Frank house, Pittsburgh, 1939. The exuberance of the furniture and interior design was considered unusual, not to say bizarre, even at the time of building. The console to the left of the wall unit housed controls to heating, lighting, and hi-fi equipment.

Fig. 160. Game room, Frank house, Pittsburgh, 1939. This was a large, open space located behind the entrance and main staircase (seen rising to the left). The use of calfskin upholstery was fashionable during the 1930s.

Fig. 161. Dressing room, Frank house, Pittsburgh, 1939. The rooms on the second floor of the house were elaborately fitted with built-in cabinetwork.

Fig. 162. Armchair, Frank house, Pittsburgh, 1939. The piece was one of a set of geometrical designs for the lounge area surrounding the fireplace on the second-floor landing.

floors, and a variety of wall coverings were used, ranging from pink-copper material designed by Anni Albers in the master bedroom to an Indian print in the guest bedroom.

The game room (fig. 160), on the ground floor just beyond the main staircase, had a dark oak parquet floor, walls of fieldstone and plaster, and furniture made from American birch and upholstered with spotted black-and-white calfskin. Beyond the game room was the swimming pool, along with various work and storage rooms.

There were at least ninety pieces of furniture specially made for the Frank house, and well over twenty lighting units, all designed by the architects. Most of the furniture was made by the New York cabinetmaking firm of Schmieg & Kotzian, while some fourteen pieces were made by Harry Meyers Co., also of New York. The furniture was specified and built during 1940 and was in place by late summer of that year.

In the Frank house the architects were undoubtedly seeking a richness and diversity of form, material, and color. All of the materials and finishes were natural ones. There was a specific and intentional contrast between the simple geometry of the house and the free and complex shapes of the furniture. All of the formal problems were posed and answered by the designers themselves. They were not imposed by the clients, whose demands were practical, not aesthetic. Breuer, who was well aware of the uniqueness of most of the Frank furniture designs, said:

> The profiles of this type of furniture give a line unprecedented in our interiors: wood in slablike forms, freely designed and even perforated in contrast to the rigid, geometric, mostly straight lines of the architecture.[90]

A contemporary critic writing in the *Architectural Forum* found that in its use of natural materials and in

the disintegration of the rectangle into freer shapes…there is a new and impressive evidence that contemporary architecture is entering a new phase, richer, more assured, and more human.[91]

The critic wrote in equally approving terms about the interiors and the built-in furniture, but not about the free-standing furniture:

> The upholstered chairs on the other hand, represent a very personal expression of taste. Essentially these pieces are a continuation of Breuer's earlier work…but the frequently extravagant shapes and bizarre combinations of material do not fulfill the promise of first expectation.

In many respects, at least in terms of the vocabulary of materials and their application to the house, the Frank house was similar to other Breuer projects and Gropius and Breuer collaborations. What made it so unusual was the lack of restraint in terms of the variety of materials and forms employed; the results did indeed appear to be extreme. The explanation for this lies partially with the elaborate program requested by the clients and the fact that the plans had to be enlarged several times during the period of design. Breuer excelled when budget restrictions were tight. In the Frank house, given virtual freedom to purchase or design whatever was desired and to experiment as he wished, he exercised little restraint. Even if we allow for differences in taste between 1939 and the present, the words bizarre and extravagant still apply to much of the interior and furniture. The furniture can best be seen in the context of Breuer's other cutout-plywood experiments.

CUTOUT-PLYWOOD FURNITURE

Breuer began designing cutout-plywood furniture after his first experiments with molded and bent plywood for Isokon. The main appeal of furniture made from pieces of plywood that needed only to be cut out with a jigsaw and then assembled was that models could be made in a small workshop, and since the furniture could be easily produced, it could be sold at a relatively low price.

Cutout plywood held a further appeal for Breuer. As he explained:

> This type of furniture represents a new principle in using plywood, which allows forms characteristic only of this material. The quality of plywood which mainly differentiates it from wood is the elimination of the structural quality of its grain. Solid wood splits and breaks along its grain. Plywood does not. It is therefore possible to cut out plywood in free forms, or to perforate it, without sacrificing its strength. It won't split under the stress, as wood will in this case. The recognition of this structural quality suggested the design of this furniture. Two cut-out plywood sides replace the usual legs, arm, and back supports, and are connected with varying seats and backs.[92]

In the earliest cutout chairs, those made in England in late 1936 (fig. 163, 164), there were problems of lateral stability. For although Breuer was right about the superior strength of plywood, the structure of the entire chair could be only as strong as the joints and connections of its various parts. The problematic design of the final version of the Isokon stacking chair (fig. 135), although it required entirely too many parts, became the starting point for the new chairs. The idea of one-piece construction for front and rear legs, seat frame, and back on each side at least reduced the number of parts, as well as the number of joints. But those fewer pieces, owing to their relative thinness, would have to be carefully designed, and a method would have to be found to connect and hold all of the elements in a solid construction.

The armchairs for the Pennsylvania Pavil-

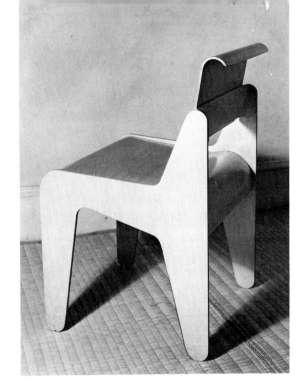

Fig. 163. Side chair, cutout plywood, made in England, 1936. Breuer constantly strove to design chairs that could be made from the smallest number of parts, preferably without necessity for large-scale factory tooling-up.

Fig. 164. Armchair, cutout plywood, made in England, 1936. Breuer designed and exhibited a very similar chair in Gropius' and his Pennsylvania Pavilion at the 1939 New York World's Fair.

ion at the 1939 World's Fair and the two-piece frame of the Bryn Mawr chair (fig. 155) were made more stable by the use of thicker side pieces and a solid seat and back, reinforced by the cross-bracing of the dowels. The result was a trimmer, more compact, and ultimately more successful chair than his experimental English models. And Breuer's argument for the use of plywood was clinched with the Frank dining chairs (fig. 158), where the strength of the side pieces in combination with dowels was sufficient to support the entire chair in a cantilevered construction. This combination permitted a different, freer shape for the side pieces. Where upholstery was added, as was the case with the Ventris chairs (fig. 148), as well as in the similar designs for the Frank house (fig. 160), the Pennsylvania Pavilion at the 1939 World's Fair (fig. 165), and Breuer's own house, an almost unlimited number of crosspieces could be added to assure stability

under the weight of sitter and upholstery framework.

In the case of the lounge chair for Heal's (fig. 138), an irregularly shaped box was made to which the upholstery and arms were applied. Strength was thereby achieved through a bulky, solid construction. The similar design for his Frank house lounge chair (fig. 159) reverted to the structural formula used for the Ventris seating. Like most of the cutout chairs, it was presented as a seat until placed between — in this case, suspended between — the two side pieces, beyond which it projected at both ends. This construction also allowed for the use of padded arms that did not have to be separately applied, as in the Heal's chair.

The structural solutions Breuer arrived at in England in 1936 for each chair type were not, therefore, substantially changed in his later American chairs. Unfortunately his aesthetic solutions similarly were little changed. Both

Fig. 165. Armchairs, Pennsylvania Pavilion, New York World's Fair, 1939. A second design exhibited at the Fair sparked widespread interest among those unfamiliar with Breuer's English furniture—and elicited comparisons with the free-form shapes of Surrealist designers, such as Frederick Kiesler, who were then prominent in the New York artistic community.

the visual characteristics and the structural problems inherent in the designs of the chairs remained. The desired simplification of the production process resulted in an oversimplification of the design of the chairs. The diagrammatic or schematic nature of the designs resulted in constructions that looked more like cardboard models of chairs than actual pieces of seating furniture. All the various chair parts, especially the important side pieces, were each cut from a single piece of plywood. (In this respect the Bryn Mawr chair was the only exception.) In order to support the chair, a relatively wide expanse of material was necessary for the side pieces. Their combination with seats and backs, which could be upholstered or solid, and were only rarely bent or molded, still led to designs in which one was always aware of the disparate parts rather than the continuous whole. The aesthetic was that of a "constructed" chair, made up of distinctly separate elements.

Inevitably these cutout pieces were flat, two-dimensional. If they were bent they had only a limited existence on another plane. No matter how intricate the pieces, no matter how organic and complicated or simple and geometrical, the effect would always be similar. No matter what the shape, the effect was that of a boxlike construction. The joining or attachments between parts were always handled at right angles. It was with good reason that the chairs were always seen in photographic views emphasizing profile or side elevations.

Breuer had come to plywood furniture as the result of Gropius' suggestion that he translate the aluminum chair into plywood. Breuer's excursions into designing organic or biomorphic forms, however, while being symptomatic of the period, and reflecting Aalto's influence, nonetheless seem to have resulted directly from his introduction to Surrealist art by Carola Giedion-Welcker, wife of Sigfried Giedion, in Zurich during the early 1930s.

Carola Giedion-Welcker wrote about and collected Arp's work, and it seems likely that she made Breuer aware of Arp's largely two-dimensional wooden sculptures or reliefs, which were executed with paper stencils.

Breuer must have realized the limitations of these designs, and, in the mid-1940s, he abandoned them to begin work on a new type of cutout-plywood furniture.

INDEPENDENT PRACTICE

Shortly after the completion of the Frank house, the partnership of Gropius and Breuer broke up. Perhaps this was inevitable. Breuer had begun his career as Gropius' student. It was Gropius' support and encouragement that had led to many of the most significant events in Breuer's professional life. It was Gropius who encouraged Breuer to stay at the Bauhaus as a teacher; Gropius who had arranged for many of Breuer's early commissions; Gropius' move to England that made possible Breuer's partnership with Yorke and the work for Isokon; and finally, Gropius who paved the way for Breuer's coming to the United States. When they established their architectural partnership in the United States, it was truly the first time the two designers—and more important, the two men—stood as equals. No longer was the relationship one of student to teacher. Their differing personalities and their very different styles of designing, plus this redefined relationship, made their parting predictable.

Breuer, at the time, was described by many as an intuitive designer. His grasp of design problems was quick, his response equally so. Gropius was a slow, some might say ponderous architect who, throughout his career, collaborated with talented younger associates who assumed much of the responsibility for design.

Gropius was the philosopher architect, the polemicist of the modern movement, always articulate on the state of the art. In contrast, Breuer was reticent about his "philosophy" of design, his view of the architectural world; his concern was design, problem solving. For Gropius the questions were always big questions; for Breuer they were of the moment, seen in relation to the situation at hand.

GELLER HOUSE

Breuer maintained his own practice in Cambridge from 1941 until 1946, at which time he moved his practice to New York, and his home first to Wellfleet on Cape Cod, and then to New Canaan, Connecticut.

His first independent commission to be built during the war years was a house for the Geller family, on Long Island. The Geller house (figs. 166–69) was a landmark of Breuer's later career and, with the exception of the Harnismacher house, was the most extensively published of his buildings. It was a "binuclear" house, based on a design idea Breuer had been working on during the preceding years, one that would be widely imitated during the next decade. He explained it in terms of "the postwar man," who

> will more than ever appreciate privacy and his intimate, complete milieu…His mechanized world, his job, will probably keep him busy not more than three or four days a week. He will naturally want to utilize his free time around the house, which ought to be a more versatile instrument…As to this design, there are two separate zones connected by an entrance hall. One is for every day's living, eating…visitors…The other one, in a separate wing, is for concentration, work, and sleeping.[93]

In the Geller house this two-part conception of public and private areas was supplemented by a guest area, adjacent to but separate from the main house.

The house was built while a wartime re-striction on domestic construction was still in effect. The Breuer design was exempted from that ban, however, and from a subsequent limitation on the dollar amount to be spent on houses built by veterans, because it was submitted to the Government as a model prefabricated house.

The Gellers agreed to Breuer's suggestion that he design furniture for the house when he explained that he had ideas for laminated-wood furniture that he had never been able to execute. A Cambridge firm, the Theodore Schwamb Company, executed his chair and table designs, while Irving & Casson, also of Cambridge, built some of the cabinetwork. The hope was that the furniture might eventually be mass-produced.

The original plans for the nine-room house (excluding the guest wing) called for forty specially designed chairs. There were actually three basic chair designs: a large lounge chair (fig. 168), a dining side chair or armchair (fig. 169), and a stacking side chair (fig. 171). In addition there were a couch, a number of large tables (fig. 193), smaller coffee (fig. 168) and bedside tables, several desks and desk-dresser units, bookcases, and other built-in cabinetwork, including a large built-in wall unit that formed part of the wall between the kitchen and dining room (fig. 169). The furniture was designed in 1945 and constructed in early 1946.

The public areas of the house, consisting of living- and dining-room spaces separated by a free-standing bookshelf unit, were both simple, open rectangular rooms, as were most of the interior spaces. The stone fireplace wall and floors offered textural contrast with the wide expanses of window and light window-framing elements. Most of the rooms were similar in feeling, although a certain variety of interior space resulted from the sloping ceilings, a consistent feature of Breuer houses of the period.

Fig. 166. Geller house, Lawrence, Long Island, 1945. Breuer's first project to be built after the severing of his partnership with Gropius, the Geller house was one of the most important and influential American houses of the 1940s.

Fig. 167. Plan, Geller house, Lawrence, Long Island, 1945. Although Breuer was certainly not the first architect to conceive of a house plan that separated public and private, or day and night, areas of the house, he was responsible for popularizing it as the "binuclear" house during the mid-1940s.

Fig. 168. Living room, Geller house, Lawrence, Long Island, 1945. One entire wall of the living room was made of rough fieldstone into which was fitted the fireplace. Breuer hoped the specially designed cutout-plywood furniture would be mass-produced someday.

Fig. 169. Dining room, Geller house, Lawrence, Long Island, 1945. In addition to the specially designed chairs and table, Breuer provided a wall unit that opened into the kitchen.

GELLER FURNITURE AND THE MUSEUM OF MODERN ART COMPETITION

The Geller house chairs represented a new direction in Breuer's furniture design. The culmination of these ideas came in the chairs he designed two years later for The Museum of Modern Art's 1948 International Competition for Low-Cost Furniture Design.[94] The competition was intended to encourage the production of affordable, well-designed furniture to fulfill the demand for such products in the burgeoning postwar housing market. Breuer's project for the competition (which in fact did not win a prize) was carried out as a "design research team" project in association with the United States Forests Products Laboratory, which provided technical assistance on materials and construction techniques.

The problems attacked in the Geller and the MoMA furniture designs were the same, the concepts of the solutions similar, although the final designs differed. An excerpt from a letter written by Breuer to Jack Pritchard neatly summarized the designer's concerns. The new furniture designs, wrote Breuer, were

> designed to side-step the high investments necessary for the laminated type of construction (like Aalto's or my Isokon designs). I wanted to avoid forms and presses to save initial costs and make changes in the designs easier. Just the same, I wanted to maintain the resiliency of the supports for greater comfort, and, in addition to this, avoid the use of front legs (as in my aluminum designs). The result is a cut-out type of furniture made out of 1½ to 2 inch thick hardwood ply with surprising resiliency.[95]

After his first experiments with simple cutout-plywood furniture, Breuer seems to have concluded that such furniture did not represent the optimum solution to the aesthetic and structural problems involved in furniture design and production. The most important design feature in modern furniture was resilience, which he believed should be achieved not through springs or heavy upholstery, but through the design and construction of the chair structure itself. As he saw it, the ideal solution would be achieved through resilience in the framing material and the use of resilient connecting members. This "ideal" solution had, of course, already been achieved in tubular steel, but public resistance to the cold and shiny material remained firm. Wood was the material that people preferred. New designs in molded laminated wood, or plywood, seemed to be the answer, since the existing cutout-plywood furniture did not satisfy the tastes of that segment of the population which purchased modern furniture. Further, existing molded-plywood chairs, including Isokon or Aalto furniture, were too expensive. The reasons for this brought Breuer to the second part of the problem, the production process, which he mentioned in the letter to Pritchard.

The production of molded-plywood furniture involved heavy initial funding for molds and presses. Further, once established, the production technique was difficult to adapt to the changing needs of the marketplace. A process was needed which did not involve substantial expenditure for initial production and which could easily be adapted to new designs or techniques.

The Isokon nesting stool (fig. 131) had served as a perfect example of a well-designed molded-plywood model with the simplest possible structure. Because of the simplicity of the design, the production costs were not excessive. But the design of the Isokon stool did not have to take into account problems of stress, resilience, and comfort. Further, it did not address the problem affecting most laminated design: that the essential reliance on supporting crosspieces, and the connections which resulted, usually weakened the chair and necessitated the use of heavier supporting frames (as had

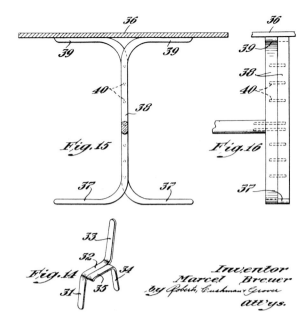

been the case in the earlier cutout-plywood chairs). This raised production costs and made satisfactory aesthetic solutions problematic. Breuer would later observe that the best molded-plywood designs did not use plywood for supporting members. Charles Eames's 1946 side chair used steel supports, as did Arne Jacobsen's 1952 stacking chair.

In his report to the MoMA competition jury, Breuer posited three requirements for a successful cutout-plywood chair:

> 1. Some wood-like or nature-textured material…which is tough and resilient, and which permits designs based on curving or bending, involving no heavy initial costs for equipment.
> 2. The number of connecting joints should be reduced to the minimum, and the remaining connections should work without weakening the members.
> 3. If possible, both members and connections should be resilient for greater comfort, and lighter in weight and appearance.[96]

Breuer attempted to meet these requirements first in the chairs he designed for the Geller house. The dining chairs (fig. 169) were made from cantilevered framing elements, two of which were placed back to back to form the leg and base of each side. Through this design Breuer achieved his goal of a chair that had no front legs, as well as one that could slide along the floor like the earlier metal furniture. Further, to the eye the elements appeared "based on curving or bending," although they were in fact cut out. The chairs were made of thick plywood that could be cut and molded in a small-scale workshop operation. The frames were resilient and, in the case of the side chairs, contained only those joinings necessary to attach the framing elements to one another and to the seat and back. (He designed a lounge chair along similar lines; it was, however, never produced.)

Breuer used a different design and construction for the large armchairs (fig. 168) and

Fig. 170. Patent drawing, table design for the Geller house, 1945. This is the basic design for the dining- and living-room tables.

Fig. 171. Stacking side chair, Geller house, Lawrence, Long Island, 1945. The compact and economical design was one of Breuer's best in cutout plywood. The house also contained examples of a larger armchair with a similar slatted seat and back.

Fig. 172. Side chair, cutout plywood, rubber
mounts, and cane, International Competition
for Low-Cost Furniture, The Museum of Modern
Art, 1948. (Collection The Museum of Modern
Art, gift of the designer.)

the stacking side chairs (fig. 171). The leg-arm units of the former and the leg-frame elements of the latter were made from thick cutout plywood which, through its open U-shape, gave resilience to the frame. The width of the frame, however, had to be increased in areas of greatest stress. The back, with its two L-shaped supports, was equally resilient. Both designs addressed the problem of minimum waste of material: the elements were cut from a board of predetermined size which yielded the largest number of parts possible.

The Geller chairs, especially the stacking chair, moved Breuer closer to an ideal solution for a laminated-wood chair. However, largely because of restrictions on the use of woods and glues due to the war, problems developed. After barely a year of use the screws that held together the frame parts of the large armchairs began to loosen. The manufacturer attributed this to the pronounced resilience of the chairs; ironically, the quality most desired had led to structural problems. And although Breuer was well aware of and had written about the problems of loose connections, he was unable to overcome them. Further, exposed to the intense sunlight that entered through the large windows of the house, the laminations of many of the chairs gradually came apart. The latter problem could, however, be solved by the use of higher-quality glues.

Despite the "bugs," the Geller armchair and, especially, the stacking chair were accomplished designs, seen in the context of Breuer's attempts to develop cutout-plywood furniture. The crucial problem that remained was how to connect the various parts so that they would be both strong and highly resilient. In his MoMA competition chairs (figs. 172–74), Breuer attempted to address the problem by completely redesigning the chairs. He further tried to reduce the thickness of the various elements, especially the leg supports, to make the chair "lighter in weight and appearance."[97] He par-

ticularly wanted the frame elements to have a uniform profile and not bulge out at the critical stress or contact points.

The new solutions arrived at in the MoMA chairs were partly the result of the research by the United States Forests Products Laboratory, acting on Breuer's request, into the structural capabilities of wood, and partly attributable to new and stronger glues and the design of a new method of connection between the various parts of the chair.

Several aspects of the chair's six-piece construction were new. The supporting members were made of one-inch bakelite-glued plywood with cross-laminations of hardwood. These additional laminations were devised to reinforce the laminated wood in both directions. The plywood was virtually indestructible after receiving the bakelite treatment. The curvilinear bends were designed to allow the stresses to flow from one member to the next; angular shapes would have reduced the strength of the chair.

The various parts were connected not only with screws, but with small pieces of rubber of varying widths. The rubber pieces were cemented between the plywood elements with a new type of rubber adhesive that was fixed by pressure and heat. The use of rubber in the joinings made the joints themselves resilient, thereby reducing the risk of breakage between any two parts.

The MoMA chair can be seen as a better-resolved version of the design first attempted in the Geller stacking chair. The use of the bakelite-treated wood and the rubber shock mounts allowed the chair to be made from more than one piece of wood on a side. Ironically, the use of the two pieces resulted in a design that was far more continuous and homogeneous in appearance than had been the Geller chairs made of fewer pieces. The added strength gained from the two pieces on each side allowed them to be thinner and

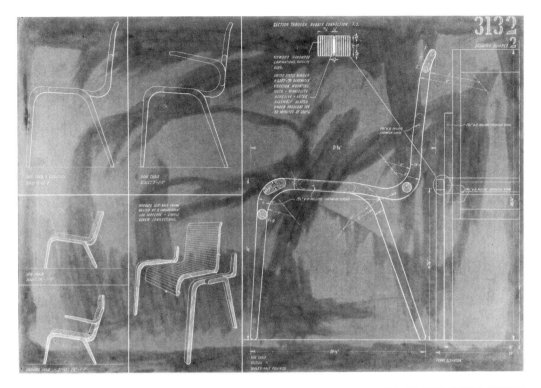

Fig. 173. Design for MoMA Competition, 1948. (Collection The Museum of Modern Art, gift of the designer.) These chair designs were developed with the research assistance of the United States Forests Products Laboratory.

Fig. 174. Design for MoMA Competition, 1948. 167 (Collection The Museum of Modern Art, gift of the designer.) The drawing of "Layout of Panels Needed for 18 Chairs" demonstrates Breuer's concern for the most efficient use of material.

more delicate in form. The disturbing thickness of the sides of the Geller chairs was thereby eliminated, replaced by gently rounded and tapered elements.

When the important cost factors were taken into consideration, the chairs would, according to Breuer, prove economical. No expensive forms or molds were required; flat plywood pieces could be cut out and glued together. There was minimal waste of material owing to the design of the parts, which used as much material as possible from every board. The use of interchangeable parts and materials in the different chair models would further reduce costs, as would the fact that the chairs could be shipped in parts and took little space to store.

LATER WORK

During the early 1950s, the volume of work produced by Breuer's office began to grow and the nature of the work began to change.[98] In 1949 an exhibition house designed by Breuer was installed in the garden of The Museum of Modern Art (fig. 175). Accompanying the exhibition was the publication of a monograph of Breuer's career to date, written by Peter Blake. Although Breuer's stature in the architectural world was already considerable, these two events enhanced his prestige and expanded the public's knowledge of his work. During the following years he received an ever-increasing number of architectural commissions. As the number of requests for large commercial buildings grew, the number of house commissions dwindled, and the designing of new furniture shrank to almost nothing. Like most architectural firms that find large projects for corporations or Government more profitable and ultimately less time-consuming than private houses, the Breuer office nonetheless usually had at least one house project going at all

times. Houses provide architects with the opportunity to show their mettle on a scale and with a directness that sometimes get lost in large projects.

The point of departure for Breuer's late houses was the planning of the binuclear Geller house, along with its treatment of material, especially the combination of large window walls and stone. With Breuer's increasing use of concrete, the combination would become one of concrete and glass.

Typical of Breuer's handling of interiors in the years to come was the use of entrance-ways separating the public and private areas of the house. Living rooms were designed as grand spaces, surrounded by wide expanses of window. Large cabinet-units were still used to define the otherwise continuously planned spaces for living and dining. The large living rooms were dominated by free-standing fireplaces — a device that would appear with increasing frequency and in bolder and more sculptural forms in later houses. Furniture was kept simple; little of it was designed by Breuer, except for a few built-in pieces. Apparently the architect was satisfied with the commercial furniture then available on the market. Designs by Eames, Saarinen, and others meant that for the first time there was well-designed modern furniture, in addition to tubular steel or Aalto plywood, readily available for purchase. This, combined with the increasing size and volume of commissions, led him largely to abandon the design of furniture except as required by clients. The only exception was his continuing design of wall units, especially those between kitchen and dining room. In some later commissions these were, however, replaced by low counters.

In 1947 Breuer built a house for himself in New Canaan (figs. 178–80). It became one of the best-known houses of the late 1940s and was one of the first designs that made the Connecticut town a mecca for aficionados of

modern architecture. The renown of the Breuer house was, however, largely eclipsed in 1949 when Philip Johnson built his own New Canaan home, a design which decisively moved away from the vernacularizing tendencies favored by Breuer and his students, toward a new formalism in design.

Breuer's house was modest in size, economical in its use of space and its low cost. The dining and living areas were just within and between the front and rear doors; two bedrooms were located off a long hallway which passed by the kitchen and bathroom. The openness of the public rooms—achieved through the clever use of partitions, the centrally located fireplace, and the lack of doors between the various spaces—made the relatively narrow house seem expansive. Further contributing to the richness of the living and dining areas were cypress boarding for the ceiling, stone and Haitian matting for the floor, white-painted plywood walls, and brick fireplace.

The simplified rectangular plan of the 1947

Fig. 175. Dining area, exhibition house, The Museum of Modern Art, 1949. For the house, Breuer made use of a sloping "butterfly" wooden ceiling, a stone floor, a number of wall units, his 1948 Competition chairs, and a table based on his 1936 English designs. The house was seen by tens of thousands of visitors while on display in the Museum garden.

Breuer house and the less-emphatic slope of it's roof contrasted with the more-intricate plans and converging slopes of the "butterfly" roofs in his double-wing binuclear houses. They signaled a new direction in his work that would become predominant during the next decade: a tendency to treat the house, and the interior spaces, as an elemental box-shape.

Four years later, in 1951, Breuer designed a second house for himself in New Canaan (fig. 181). In it, as in other houses of the period, he used a now-familiar vocabulary of materials that offered a variety of textures, colors, and patterns: the floor was an irregular pattern of waxed split-stone, the ceiling was composed of horizontal wooden boards, and the walls were either rough stone, painted in a light

color, or glass, the latter punctuated by richly stained wooden pillars.

The second Breuer New Canaan house was large, with four bedrooms. The basic arrangement of dining and living spaces opening into each other was maintained, but a new element was added: with the fireplace located against an exterior living-room wall, a bamboo screen was used to divide living and dining areas. A visitor entering the house immediately walked by a bedroom and was able to see most of the various elements of the plan: public areas directly ahead and to the right and a corridor leading down to the other bedrooms. In certain respects, the plan remained a binuclear one.

Several other design elements, all of which

Fig. 176. Tompkins house, Hewlett Harbor, Long Island, 1945. The Windsor-type rocking chair seemed particularly appropriate sitting in front of the large open hearth in what has always appeared to be a particularly American tableu. Other chairs in the house were designed by Alvar Aalto and Bruno Matthson.

had existed previously in Breuer's domestic work, became more and more important in his American houses. His much-admired staircases (fig. 152) were employed as transparent, often cantilevered objects in space. With their emphatically diagonal shapes for the frames and banisters, as well as the necessarily rigid horizontal treads, the staircases became dramatic constructions, articulated in skeletal fashion for maximum effect. They became a device which could connect different spaces and levels of the house while remaining distinctly separate, enlivening the overall design of exterior or interior.

Another important device in his later interiors was the fireplace, which gradually became one of the most dramatic and conspicuous elements within the overall interior designs. Breuer had begun to make fireplaces of rough fieldstone in the 1930s; in certain houses — in his own Lincoln house or the later Geller house (fig. 168), for example — they were incorporated into large stone walls. Increasingly, however, Breuer came to treat the fireplace as a plastic element in space, projecting from the wall, or even free-standing. In the Chamberlain cottage (fig. 154) or Tompkins house (fig. 176), it became not only a free-standing divider of interior spaces, but also a sculptural object, the emphatic focus of a large room. In the Robinson house, the fireplace (fig. 177) was perforated and oriented toward the large, open window-wall, the dense, sculptural mass providing a striking contrast to the openness of the interior space, which was surrounded on three sides by large window-walls. One could see not only through the cutout at the top of the fireplace, but also through the hearth. Although Breuer continued to use the fireplace as a divider of spaces, it became more regularized as a shape and was usually made of white-painted brick, as in his first New Canaan home (fig. 179). Many of the fireplaces of this period were, owing to the shapes

and the relationship of hearth to chimney, reminiscent of Le Corbusier's fireplaces of the 1930s.

Beginning in the mid-1950s, Breuer's treatment of the fireplace became even bolder and more sculptural, although the results were not always as successful or as well integrated into the overall interior design as they had been earlier. In the Starkey house (fig. 182), for example, the effect of the large mass of the fireplace was somewhat diminished by the irregular shapes cut into it. A softer, more abstract shape was fitted into the lower space of the Gagarin living room (fig. 183), offering an emphatic contrast of form and texture to the regularized container of the house and the richly stained wooden floors and ceilings. The

Fig. 177. Fireplace, Robinson house, Williamstown, Mass., 1947. The unusual granite fireplace was placed close to the window wall in the large living room.

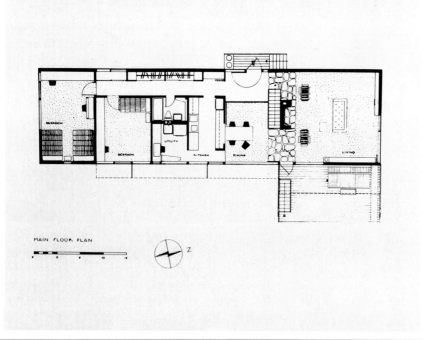

MAIN FLOOR PLAN

Fig. 178. Breuer house I, New Canaan, 1947. The house, which sat on a hillside, was framed and clad in wood and raised on a concrete base. On some walls the exterior wood planking was laid diagonally for reinforcement.

Fig. 179. Plan, Breuer house I, New Canaan, 1947.

Fig. 180. Breuer house I, New Canaan, 1947. View from the living room into the dining area. The radio cabinet, dining table, and of course the chairs were all designed by Breuer.

Fig. 181. Breuer house II, New Canaan, 1951. View from the living room into the dining area. The entrance and cloakroom are to the left. The house was not wood-framed, but constructed of rough masonry slabs.

use of an abstract shape—not unlike the contemporary sculptures of Isamu Noguchi—was carried over, but on a much larger scale, into the McMullen beach house (fig. 184). The importance Breuer gave to the fireplace, indeed, its complete domination of the interior space, suggested an architectural vision related to the scale, shape, and texture of his large concrete buildings. Breuer's interiors tended to become more and more dominated by masonry, which he increasingly used for floors as well as fireplaces. Within the simplified geometrical shapes of his houses, the masonry elements created a compelling textural effect which, when combined with large, uncluttered interior spaces, resulted in a new sense of monumentality.

Around 1953, following the first of Le Corbusier's celebrated poured-concrete buildings, Breuer began serious investigations into the structural possibilities of concrete, which he applied, for the most part, to large commissions, such as office or public buildings. But this interest also showed itself in his fireplaces and, in certain instances, his furniture design. In 1951 he had designed for his New Canaan home an outdoor table (fig. 185), which recalled his glass-brick table for the Frank house (fig. 186). This innocent gesture, a pile of cinder blocks arranged on a stone floor, supporting a large stone top, revealed a change in attitude that did not become evident in his buildings for several years. Masonry, in whatever form, became increasingly important in his work. He became enthralled with the texture and feel of concrete and stone and, above all, with its stability, solidity, and permanence. The man who had begun his career designing furniture which, above all else, was to express lightness, mobility, and transpar-

Fig. 182. Breuer with Herbert Beckhard and Robert Gatje, Starkey house, Duluth, Minn., 1954–55. Breuer increasingly made his fireplaces in bushhammered concrete. The house was dramatically sited overlooking Lake Superior.

Fig. 183. Breuer with Herbert Beckhard, Gagarin house, Litchfield, Conn., 1954. Teak floors, thick carpets, wooden beams, glass walls, and the concrete fireplace all demonstrated Breuer's interest in texture.

Fig. 184. Breuer with Herbert Beckhard, McMullen beach house, Mantoloking, N.J., 1960. Another bushhammered concrete fireplace, here installed in a large, two-story living room.

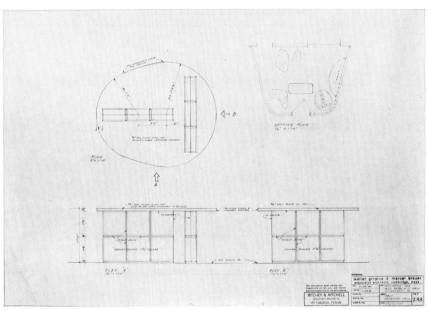

Fig. 185. Outdoor table, concrete blocks with stone top, 1951. Standing outside Breuer's second New Canaan home, the table symbolized the architect's interest in monumental masonry forms.

Fig. 186. Drawing, glass-brick table, entrance hall, Frank house, Pittsburgh, 1939. (Collection Busch-Reisinger Museum, Harvard University.) This is an early instance of Breuer's interest in what he termed "built furniture."

ency, was now, in his mature years, developing a new aesthetic. The permanence, the monumentality of the stone table, of the large fireplace, of the building itself, came to hold a fascination for Breuer.

His late domestic interiors, such as the large arched space of the second Geller house (fig. 187), with its stone floors and concrete fireplace wall, provided the backdrop for Breuer's massive polished-granite tables and counters. The smooth texture and elemental structure of these designs were the more elegant expression of the ideas prefigured in the tables for the Frank house and his New Canaan home.

Breuer's fascination with furniture as solid and sculptural as his later buildings was seen especially in the interior furnishings he provided for churches, convents, and synagogues, where a monumental type of design was particularly appropriate. The altars, lecterns, communion tables, and abbot's throne of St. John's Abbey (fig. 188), for example, were conceived of as sculptures in bushhammered concrete with granite. The rows of wooden choir stalls, sheltered by low masonry walls, created the form and outline for the "stage" of the sanctuary.

Despite Breuer's interest in these designs, he still designed less-imposing furniture for certain contexts. The deck of his own New Canaan house of 1947 had a built-in table with benches (fig. 189)—a modest but successful design. For his second New Canaan house, 1951, he devised a writing desk (fig. 190) that looked back to his earliest furniture designed in a constructivist spirit, with ele-

Fig. 187. Breuer with Herbert Beckhard, Geller house II, Lawrence, Long Island, 1967–69. Although the house was based on an earlier design of 1959, it was furnished with Breuer's monumental granite tables and counters, which became common in his late houses and even in commissions for offices.

ments floating in space, projecting from a framework of thin, crisscrossing wooden parts. He also continued to use wall units in a variety of shapes and sizes. And he designed a large-scale seating plan for his Sarah Lawrence Arts Center (fig. 191) of 1950–52, where rows of chairs were attached to long tube-steel bases, which allowed for mobility. In this instance, Breuer's use of thin, black-painted steel tubing for chair frames was typical of the 1950s, as was the design of the bases, which owed something to the wire furniture of Eames and Harry Bertoia.

Breuer's B32 side chair, since 1960 usually referred to as the "Cesca" chair, became the object of renewed attention at that time. Breuer, as well as many other architects, began to use it extensively beginning in the late '50s, when it again became widely available. But for a house he designed in Switzerland, Breuer, with his partner Herbert Beckhard, provided a group of dining chairs (fig. 192) that were far more closely related to historical furniture than had been any of his earlier designs. He chose an X-shaped base, a form that recalled the crossed-support stools and chairs used from ancient times to the Renaissance, and recalled as well Mies van der Rohe's famous Barcelona chair (1929) and several popular lounge chairs of the 1950s. Unfortunately Breuer's use of an X-shaped base was not well integrated with the seat and back. The base design was more successful in the dining tables, which were similar to Breuer's designs of 1945–46 for the Geller house (fig. 170).

Fig. 188. Breuer with Hamilton Smith, sanctuary, St. John's Abbey, Collegeville, Minn., 1953–61. Part of an entire Abbey University complex built by the Breuer office from 1953 to 1968, the interior spaces and furnishings reflected the scale of the exterior, one of Breuer's most dramatic concrete structures.

Fig. 189. Terrace, Breuer house I, New Canaan, 1947. Marcel Breuer and his wife Constance—they were married in 1940—sitting at the built-in table and benches on the terrace of their first New Canaan home.

Fig. 190. Desk, wood, 1951. Designed for the second New Canaan Breuer house and often referred to as the "New Canaan Desk," the piece was mass-produced for several years by Gavina of Milan.

Fig. 191. Auditorium seating, Arts Center, Sarah Lawrence College, Bronxville, N.Y., 1950–52.

Fig. 192. Breuer with Herbert Beckhard, chairs and tables, Koerfer house, Switzerland, 1963–67.

180

Conclusion

Marcel Breuer's contribution to the development of modern furniture and interior design
has been a decisive one. Despite his Bauhaus
education, which espoused an equality of all
the arts, and despite the view held since the
late nineteenth century that the hierarchy of
the arts—with easel painting at the top and
interior design close to the bottom—should
be abandoned, Breuer would undoubtedly
prefer that any discussion of his career center
on his architectural work, especially his later
buildings. The singular importance of his early
work makes that an impossibility.

The extent of Breuer's achievement by the
age of twenty-eight was one of the most remarkable aspects of his career. For if we knew
only what he accomplished up to 1930, it
would still remain one of the most significant
bodies of work in twentieth-century design. In
the 1920s Breuer's youth worked distinctly to
his advantage—he was born at the right time.
Unlike architects already trained in one tradition of design who switched their allegiance
to a modern aesthetic, Breuer was of the age
where he was able to become completely
educated in the precepts of the newly developing modernism. His lack of prior training or
substantive artistic background allowed his
Bauhaus education—with its emphasis on the
mastery of craft—to shape the young artist.
He approached his design work with an originality of conception and freedom of mind
nurtured by Bauhaus ideals. He was fortunate

in being recognized by Gropius and other Bauhäusler and in being given the opportunity to work so extensively on furniture and interiors at the Bauhaus at so early an age.

His earliest designs—those done up to 1925—were highly accomplished examples of student work produced under the influence of international constructivism and, especially, Dutch de Stijl. Polemically oriented and manifestolike in its dogmatism, the student work was strongly tied to a certain point in the history of artistic thought. Not so the work he designed in a burst of creative energy between 1925 and 1930. In these designs he created furniture and interiors which, half a century later, remain as modern and contemporary, as vital and relevant, as anything designed in our own time.

Breuer's development of tubular-steel furniture was revolutionary. His prototypical furniture provided the basis for hundreds of tubular-steel designs that appeared all over Europe and the United States during the 1920s and '30s. In tubular steel Breuer had found a perfect solution to the problem of chair design. Tubular steel was, and is, a unique material for mass-produced furniture. No other substance offered comparable strength, resilience, lightness, comfort, or resistance to wear or damage. Tubular steel could overcome the limitations imposed on the design and manufacture of virtually any other material. It was uniquely suited to the modern interior and to modern methods of mass production. And few tubular-steel designs became as popular or as emblematic of the machine-oriented aesthetic of the period as Breuer's steel, wood, and cane armchair, the B32 side chair, or his minimal B9 stool.

At the same time that Breuer designed his new tubular-steel furniture, he arrived at distinguished solutions to the problems of interior design. He concentrated on a narrow range of materials and furniture types. He developed only a few basic designs in wood for tables and wall storage units. With great sensitivity and clarity he created interior designs through the use of a small number of component elements, allowing each, whether it was a woven floor covering, a wide expanse of wall, or a piece of furniture, to assume large significance within the interior space he had conceived. And although his vocabulary changed through the years, the principles and the results were, for the most part, the same in his later work.

Throughout his career Breuer was resolute in his search for comfort in furniture. He considered resilience the single most important structural feature in seating furniture. Comfort was to be achieved through the actual design of his chairs, not through the application of upholstery or padding to stiff frames. After his pioneer work with tubular steel, he experimented with aluminum and plywood, seeking to come to terms with other materials suitable for mass production. He readily accepted the challenge of designing less-expensive furniture that might be acceptable to a public still disdainful of the use of tubular steel in the domestic interior. In his later plywood models, some of which were among his least successful designs, he sought to make possible the production of modern furniture without the large pre-production investments necessary for most furniture manufacturing.

Despite the historical significance and, at certain times, the popularity of some of Breuer's furniture designs, few of them were ever produced in the quantity and at the low cost envisioned by the designer. In 1948, after considerable experience, he was able to observe:

> Most modern designers interested in the scope and social aspects of their work, try to create a piece of furniture which can be truly mass produced. What actually happens is that mass production never gets started; the furniture specifically designed for mass pro-

duction is produced in relatively small quantities, sold for a relatively higher price, and by reason of this higher price never creates the great public demand which would justify its truly low cost mass production.[99]

With the exception of his tubular-steel chairs, which were still expensive in comparison with simple bentwood furniture, few of Breuer's designs actually achieved commercial success. It was only in the 1960s that his B32 chair became relatively inexpensive (through lower-quality copies) and widely popular. Ironically, this occurred at a time when Breuer had all but given up the design of furniture, especially furniture suitable for mass production.

Marcel Breuer's furniture designs, especially his work in tubular steel, constitute one of the most impressive achievements in modern design. Through his intuitive sense of design and his intimate knowledge of materials, he was able to create furniture and interiors that rose above the level of decoration or function and achieved a beauty and timelessness that put them among the significant accomplishments of twentieth-century art.

APPENDIX 1
TUBULAR-STEEL DESIGNS MISATTRIBUTED TO BREUER

Beginning in 1930 the Thonet company produced a number of tubular-steel furniture models that carried a designer credit for Marcel Breuer. With the exception of models B15 and B15a, the designs discussed below never appeared in Breuer's contracts with Thonet, nor was he ever paid royalties on the designs; and in interviews conducted for this book Breuer denied ever having designed them. Not included in this tally are models that were minor variations of Breuer designs often credited to him, or models which, although never credited by Thonet to Breuer, were clearly based on his designs; among the latter must be included many tubular-steel beds and all of the tubular-steel theater seating units, with the exception of Breuer's original B1 (fig. 29).

The most problematic of these designs were the reclining couches B15 and B15a (fig. 193). Model B15 was clearly the design of Kalman Lengyel, the cofounder of Standard-Möbel, and was labeled as such in the second Standard-Möbel catalog. Thonet produced a variant with an adjustable back, B15a, which may have been Breuer's idea but was hardly an original design. Thonet paid royalties to Breuer for both models during the 1930s.

The stool B8 illustrated here (fig. 194) was one of several models that were at different times sold as B8. The first model B8 was a folding side chair (fig. 47) the second was a B9 stool with soft fabric seat; both were designed by Breuer. A later model was an adaptation by the Thonet company of Breuer's B27 table base (fig. 74) to a small stool. Thonet also produced it with caned seat as model B56 (fig. 194). The base was briefly used in the production of chair models B5 and B11.

Armchair B36 (fig. 197) has always seemed an unlikely Breuer design, and despite its carrying the credit "Arch. Marcel Breuer" it was not a Breuer design; nor was the table B53 (fig. 195). The B63 ottoman (fig. 196) was designed by Thonet to complement Breuer's B25 lounge chair; Breuer himself never used the chair with the ottoman. Desks B65 (fig. 198) and B465, although based on the B21 typing table (fig. 74) and among the more interesting tubular-steel desks of the period, also were not Breuer designs. Finally, the B114 bar stool (fig. 199) was credited to Breuer in the first Thonet catalogs, but later the attribution was given to the French designer Emile Guillot.

The reasons for the confusion surrounding these designs are several. Occasionally, the pieces were shown in catalog pictures with other Breuer furniture, and the designer credit at the bottom of the photograph was mistakenly thought to refer to all of the designs in the photograph. In other cases, it seems apparent that Thonet used the credit as a selling device to enhance the prestige of a design that was being directed at a fairly sophisticated market well aware of the various architect-designers. Finally, in certain cases, it is quite possible that a given design represented at least some of Breuer's ideas, and although Breuer did not feel the design was his, the Thonet company felt at liberty to use Breuer's name.

APPENDIX 2
THE HOUSE INTERIOR
BY MARCEL BREUER

From a lecture given by Breuer at the Technical University, Delft, 1931, published in a slightly different form in the German magazine *Bauwelt* (7 May 1931).

The crucial formation of the new home finds its initial solution from within, in other words, from the interior.

The deciding factors for the shaping of the interior, their basis, and their intrinsic possibilities, rest in the house itself — in its interior and total organization, in its floor plan, in its "architecture." In the ideal (or more properly stated, the correct) situation, the interior is no longer an independent unit set into the house, but is constructively tied to the building itself — properly speaking, it begins with the floor plan, rather than after the completion of the building, as was earlier the case.

Only the ideal situation allows for this organic unity: that is, the completely furnished new construction. In practice, it is more often the case that existing homes are redecorated with a fresh viewpoint: something that is entirely feasible even though it does not allow for a complete solution.

It is incorrect to identify a lack of ornament as the difference between the new room and the more traditional room, as people generally do. Angular rooms without ornament or moldings are generally considered to be characteristic of the modern movement, the "modern style." Colloquially, the term "Neue Sachlichkeit" [New Objectivity] is used — which is an error in our view.

Today's production of flat facades and furniture without relief or embellishment is in no way better or more lovely than the worst products of the '90s. The aforementioned trademarks are not characteristic of our work. On the contrary, I consider them to be of second-

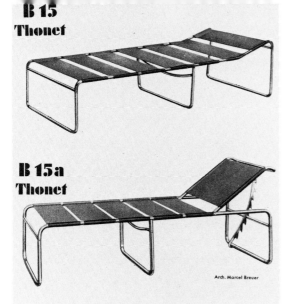

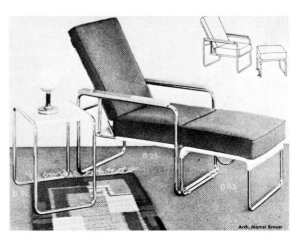

Fig. 193

Fig. 194

Fig. 195

Fig. 196

Fig. 197

Fig. 198

Fig. 199

Fig. 193. Thonet chaises longues B15 and B15a.
Fig. 194. Thonet stools B8 and B56.
Fig. 195. Table B53, seen with Breuer's B34½ armchair.
Fig. 196. Ottoman B63, illustrated with Breuer's B25 lounge chair and B9c nesting table.

Fig. 197. Thonet armchair B36.
Fig. 198. Desk B65, illustrated with an armchair version of Breuer's B7a and E. W. Buquet's adjustable architect's lamp.
Fig. 199. Thonet bar stool B114.

ary importance. We have no desire to present a purely formal point of view; instead, we see our mission in creating a home that is simpler, lighter, more comfortable in a biological sense, and independent of exterior factors.

This development places the following problem in the foreground: The necessity for the utmost economy in space demands a machine for living, which must actually be constructed like a machine, with engineering developments and the latest in mechanization.

Practically speaking: Everything is either built-in or permanent, every object is placed in a specific location—beds, tables, collapsible night tables, everything measured off in the smallest dimensions and interlocking. Maximum use of space, as in a ship's cabin or a train compartment. The individual life functions must be intensively analyzed and taken into account as much as possible. The house, in other words, should be based on the body.

Here it must be emphasized, however, that these various solutions present possible dangers, such as: oppressive, imperfectly functioning, or fragile machines in the daily environment; addiction to function; petty concern over details…all aesthetically unsettling, disturbing results of ineffectual striving. A pompous overconstruction—*l'art pour l'art*.

Despite intensive investigation of the life functions, we must achieve a few general—at least relatively general—forms.

Basically: A few simple objects are enough, when these are good, multiuse, and capable of variation. We avoid thus the slavish pouring of our needs into countless commodities that complicate our daily lives instead of simplifying them and making them easier. For example: An ordinary chair does not need to be adjustable for various sizes of people. The problem, although initially tempting, is not significant enough to make all of the complications worthwhile. Or: Only in the rarest cases does a bed need to be folded up for lack of space. One can design it so that it provides seating and lounging space during the day—which also eliminates the need for extra chairs.

Another solution is to build in as few furnishings as possible, creating multiple-use units instead. These can be put next to one another or on top of one another, depending upon their intended use and the dimensions of the room.

Such units should be standard, so that they can be combined. The goal must be not to produce a finished model complete in itself, but rather to produce basic units that can be combined and recombined at any time. The result is furniture that is independent because it has the simplest form, furniture with no composition—neither beginning nor end—that can also be secondary, part of a yet undetermined continuation. This principle applies particularly to closets and all cupboards in the house.

What is true of the permanently fixed cupboard is not true of the actual furniture, i.e., chairs, beds, and tables. These should be good, well-formed, independent models, whose main characteristics are mobility, lightness, and where possible, transparency.

Regarding the artificial lighting of a room the following must be said: Out with traditional ornamental lighting fixtures, with complicated modern or old-fashioned chandeliers, etc.! I find the trivial and endless variation in this area petty and tiring. The light fixture interests me only insofar as it is an unavoidably necessary instrument and the carrier of light.

Two types of lighting can be clearly distinguished: spot lighting and general room lighting. For the first, table or wall arms with as many joints as possible should be used, with the same lamp serving as many purposes as possible (on the desk, bed, etc.). For general room lighting, the most desirable light is indirect lighting, mounted on the walls or on low cabinets, flooding the ceiling and thereby the room with one-sided indirect light. In this area, our assignment is not the design of the lighting fixture, but rather the shaping of the light itself.

There has seldom been a more misunderstood concept than colorfulness or "joy in color" in architecture. Following in the steps of the modern movement came a shocking brightness, a substitute for arts and crafts, which offended anyone who did not look at colors with his eyes closed, in other words, anyone who looked at color as more than a principle. I consider "white" a very versatile and beautiful color; at the same time it is the brightest color—there is seldom a reason to replace it with any other color. Living things appear more intense in bright monochromatic rooms, and this is important to me. The decorations in such rooms are the tools of daily life, man himself—and the best ornaments of all: plants. Simply stated: The home should be neither a color composition nor a spiritual self-portrait of its architect!

Translated by Kathleen Fluegel

NOTES

1. Although Breuer has always cited his birthdate as 22 May, several documents from his personal files, dating from 1926 and 1929, refer to his birthdate as 21 May 1902. Marcel Breuer Collection, George Arents Research Library for Special Collections, Syracuse University, Box 10. (The Breuer Collection is not yet cataloged; therefore references cannot always be made to specific files.)

2. In 1926, Breuer filed papers with the Official Provincial Rabbinate (Amtliches Landesrabbinat) in Dessau declaring that he did not wish to be considered Jewish. Breuer Collection, Box 10.

3. Forbat also went to the Bauhaus in 1920; there he taught part-time while working in Gropius' architectural office.

4. Letter from Gropius to Peter Blake, 10 Jan. 1949; Breuer correspondence file, Department of Architecture and Design, MoMA.

5. Walter Gropius, "Die Entwicklung moderner Industriebaukunst," *Jahrbuch des deutschen Werkbundes*, 1913, translated in Tim and Charlotte Benton with Dennis Sharp, *Architecture and Design 1890–1939* (New York: Whitney Library of Design, 1975), p. 53 (hereafter cited as Benton).

6. Letter from Fritz Mackensen to Walter Gropius, 14 Oct. 1915, translated in Hans M. Wingler, *The Bauhaus* (Cambridge, Mass.: M.I.T. Press, 1976), p. 22 (hereafter as Wingler).

7. Letter from Gropius to Mackensen, 19 Oct. 1915, Wingler, p. 22.

8. Gropius, "Recommendations for the Founding of an Educational Institution as an Artistic Counseling Service for Industry, the Trades, and the Crafts," Wingler, p. 23.

9. Translated in Wingler, p. 31.

10. Marcel Franciscono, *Walter Gropius and the Creation of the Bauhaus Weimar* (Urbana: University of Illinois Press, 1971), pp. 88 ff. (hereafter as Franciscono).

11. Quoted in Hans Eckstein, "purpose and goal of workshop education at the bauhaus," in *50 Years Bauhaus* (Toronto: Art Gallery of Ontario, 1969), p. 75. The use of only lowercase letters in publications written by Bauhäusler (Bauhaus students or teachers) was consistent with the new style of typography (which also included the strict use of sanserif lettering) championed by Herbert Bayer and adopted by the Bauhaus beginning in 1925.

12. All direct or indirect quotations of Breuer that are not attributed to a specific source are from a series of interviews conducted by the author between 1978 and 1980. Despite Breuer's account of his late arrival, it is possible that when he arrived the course was not yet part of the school's curriculum. It was not mentioned in the first Bauhaus Program, and descriptions of it did not appear until October 1920, by which time Breuer was at the Bauhaus. It seems likely, however, that Itten was teaching some form of the course shortly after his arrival in 1919. Cf. Franciscono, p. 174.

13. Peter Blake, *Marcel Breuer: Architect and Designer* (New York: MoMA, 1949), p. 15 (hereafter as Blake).

14. A surviving drawing for the entrance hall does not show Breuer's chairs, but more traditional furniture and an arrangement which was not used in the house when it was built. The drawing is published in Wingler, p. 239, where the date of the house is mistakenly given as 1921.

15. Franciscono, p. 243.

16. Van Doesburg quoted in Ludwig Grote, "basic form and functionalism," in *50 Years Bauhaus*, p. 18.

17. Theodore M. Brown, *The Work of G. Rietveld, Architect* (Utrecht: Bruna & Zoon, 1958), p. 31.

18. In June 1922, Oskar Schlemmer reflected Corbusier's influence when he wrote: "we need living machines instead of cathedrals—let us turn away, therefore, from the middle ages and from the concept of craftsmanship…" Quoted in *50 Years Bauhaus*, p. 20.

19. *50 Years Bauhaus*, p. 314.

20. Herbert Bayer, Walter and Ise Gropius, *Bauhaus 1919–1928* (New York: MoMA, 1938), p. 25.

21. Letter from Lyonel Feininger to Julia Feininger, 5 Oct. 1922, translated in Wingler, p. 56.

22. *Bauhaus 1919–1928*, p. 25.

23. The table is traditionally said to have received the Parsons name because Jean-Michel Frank, with whom many associated the design, taught at the Parsons school in Paris.

24. *Bulletin de L'Effort Moderne*, no. 9 (Nov. 1924), n.p. A record of the trip exists in a letter written by Breuer to his colleague Erich Dieckmann, published in Karl Heinz Hüter, *Das Bauhaus in Weimar* (Berlin: Akademie Verlag, 1976), pp. 276–77.

25. From the manuscript of the English translation of Ise Gropius' diary; entry for 27 Nov. 1926.

26. A similiar association with the bicycle was made by Le Corbusier at precisely the same time when he wrote of the staircase in his 1925 Pavillon de l'Esprit Nouveau: "We have made a staircase like a bicycle frame." From Le Corbusier, *Almanach d'Architecture*

Moderne (Paris: Les Editions G. Cres et Cie, 1925), p. 145, cited in Sigfried Giedion, *Mechanization Takes Command* (New York: Norton, 1969), p. 492.

27. From "metallmöbel," printed in Werner Gräff, ed., *Innenräume* (Stuttgart: Fr. Wedekind, 1928), p. 134, and translated in Benton, p. 227. At least one Bauhäusler, Andrew Weininger, recalls seeing Breuer's first designs in tubular aluminum.

28. Although the newspaper has not been traced, Breuer clearly recalls its publication; it was the reason he was not allowed to patent the design, since German patent law proscribes the patenting of a design that has previously been published.

29. Translated in Benton, p. 226.

30. The naming of the chair was the idea of Dino Gavina of Milan, who began reproducing the Breuer designs in 1960.

31. *Mechanization Takes Command*, p. 493. The extensive use of horsehair was clearly recalled by several Bauhäusler

32. Published in *Bauhaus Journal 1926*, no. 1, p. 3, and translated in Wingler, p. 424.

33. The Kandinsky bedroom furniture was never photographed, and until her death in 1980, was still used by Nina Kandinsky in her Paris apartment. The bed, stools, and night table were virtually all made from round pieces of wood.

34. Many of the rooms in the Gropius house were fitted with interesting built-in cabinetwork which was not well photographed, but which was illustrated in Walter Gropius, *Bauhausbauten Dessau* (Bauhaus book no. 12) (Munich: Albert Langen Verlag, 1930), the best source for illustrations of Bauhaus buildings.

35. German design registration 96,4585, 13 Sept. 1926 and 25 Mar. 1927, also filed as a patent in France, no. 640,760, 12 Sept. 1927. Breuer registered the design since he was unable to patent the new chairs because of their publication in 1925. A design registration was an alternative form of protection that covered "models of utility," offered initial protection of three years, as opposed to fifteen in a patent, and included designs where "no real technical effect was required...any substantially new useful effect being sufficient." It therefore measured novelty only in terms of utility. An ancillary form of protection was available in an artistic copyright, which covered only the "artistic or aesthetic effect ...[of] industrial models or designs." The two forms of protection could be used to cover a single design. (When Mart Stam designed his cantilevered chair [see below, p. 70], he applied for an artistic copyright.) Design registrations technically could not be granted for designs that had been previously published, but unlike patent applications, they entailed no elaborate examination of the validity of an application. A design registration could be challenged only by an infringement action. Quotations from Emerson Stringham, ed., *Patents and Gebrauchsmuster in International Law* (Madison, Wis.: Pacot Publications, 1935), pp. 195–221.

36. Ise Gropius diary, entry for 13 Feb. 1926.

37. Ise Gropius diary, entry for 24 Mar. 1927.

38. The use of the letter *B* to designate Breuer furniture did indeed refer to the designer's name but had its origins in the Thonet company's labeling system, initiated in 1925–26, which used letters to designate furniture types. A simple bentwood side chair was model A14, an armchair, B14. Standard-Möbel's use of a similar designation must have represented a conscious reference to the famous maker of bentwood furniture.

39. A similar leg profile was used in a 1927 round table designed by Gustav Hassenpflug, a Bauhaus student who studied with and later worked as an assistant to Breuer. The design was later sold by the Swiss design store Wohnbedarf, although the firm printed the table without a design credit. It was later used, in a slightly modified form, as a dining table by Walter and Ise Gropius in their Lincoln, Mass., home, where it still remains. See *Bauhaus 1919–1928*, p. 127.

40. Le Corbusier, *Towards a New Architecture* (New York: Praeger, 1972), pp. 114–15 (hereafter as Le Corbusier).

41. According to correspondence in the Mies van der Rohe Archive, MoMA, Breuer had expressed interest in designing one of the houses. After his offer was rejected, Gropius urged his participation through the design of several interiors.

42. He wrote about this in his essay in *Innenräume*, p. 133; this section of the essay was omitted from the translation in Benton cited above.

43. Advertisement printed in *Bauhaus Journal 1928*, no. 1, and translated in Wingler, p. 452.

44. This and the three following extracts are from Breuer's "Metallmöbel und moderne räumlichkeit," *Das Neue Frankfurt* vol. 2, no. 1 (1928), pp. 11–12, translated in *50 Years Bauhaus*, p. 109.

45. Muche, "Fine Art and Industrial Form," from the first issue of the *Bauhaus Journal 1926*, translated in Benton, p. 152.

46. Le Corbusier, p. 221.

47. From "metallmöbel," in Benton, p. 226.

48. Le Corbusier, p. 222.

49. This and the two following extracts are from John Gloag, "Wood or Metal?" *The Studio,* vol. 97 (1929), pp. 49–50.

50. Maurice Dufrêne, "A Survey of Modern Tendencies in Decorative Art," *The Studio Yearbook of Decorative Art* (London: Studio, 1931), pp. 2–4.

51. Aldous Huxley, "Notes on Decoration," *Creative Art,* no. 4 (Oct. 1930), p. 242.

52. "metallmöbel," in Benton, p. 226.

53. The meeting was described in Heinz Rasch, "Aus den zwanziger Jahren," *Werk und Zeit,* vol. 9, no. 11 (Nov. 1960), pp. 1–3. In attendance were Stam, Mies, Rasch, and Le Corbusier.

54. Information in this section is based on the personal files of Anton Lorenz, now in the possession of his former business partner Peter Fletcher of Boynton Beach, Florida, and on material in the Breuer Collection.

55. All quotations in this paragraph are from a transcript of the Appeals Court decision (Appeal of the decision of the 10th Civil Senate of the Supreme Court at Berlin, 22 Apr. 1931, proclaimed on 27 Feb. 1932, damages set on 1 June 1932), Breuer Collection.

56. In a subsequent court suit initiated by the Mauser company, manufacturers of tubular-steel furniture, against Mies and Lorenz, Mauser attempted to prove that a designer named Stüttgen had designed the first tubular-steel cantilevered chair in 1925. The claim was rejected in the original suit and twice on appeal, the last time in 1940, after Lorenz had left Nazi Germany. Lorenz and his associates felt that Stüttgen's story was a fabrication, since no proof could be offered and the testimony was entirely unconvincing. (Lorenz papers.)

57. This included Lorenz' freely plagiarizing Breuer's early tubular-steel designs, even those which were registered, for his new DESTA company, which manufactured Breuer's B9, B12, B22, B23, B27, and B14.

58. When the design was reproduced beginning in the 1960s, Breuer shortened the arms, which he, and others, found somewhat ungainly.

59. Ise Gropius diary, entry for 27 Nov. 1926.

60. These conflicts were noted by Ise Gropius in her diary entry for 16 Dec. 1926, and independently recalled by Andrew Weininger.

61. Ise Gropius diary, entry for 6 Apr. 1927.

62. Sibyl Moholy-Nagy, *Moholy-Nagy: Experiment in Totality* (Cambridge, Mass: M.I.T. Press, 1969), p. 46.

63. Ise Gropius diary, 21 May 1927.

64. Sibyl Moholy-Nagy, p. 46.

65. See Appendix 2.

66. Ibid.

67. "L'Union des Artistes Modernes au Pavillon de Marsan," *Art et Industrie* (July 1930), vol. 6, no. 7, p. 26, translated on p. 46.

68. *Journal des Debats* (10 June 1930), cited in *Bauhaus 1919–1928,* p. 94.

69. See Appendix 2.

70. Ibid.

71. Lecture, "Where Do We Stand?" reprinted in Blake, p. 119.

72. From the English patent (416,758) "Spring Seat and Reclining Chair," filed 20 Nov. 1933; adapted from the original German patent of 22 Nov. 1932.

73. From "die ferdernde aluminiumstühle von marcel breuer, budapest," and "Schweizer Aluminium Moebel," unpublished multipage descriptions of the aluminum furniture, Breuer Collection, Box 10.

74. English patent 416,758.

75. Ibid.

76. Letter 12 Dec. 1934, Breuer to L. & C. Arnold, Arnold File, Box 10, Breuer Collection.

77. In 1942 Breuer is known to have worked on aluminum furniture once again, but no photographs survive. In a description for Jack Pritchard, he wrote:
    "Maintaining the idea of the split bar, together with the idea of springing type resilient supports, I tried to make improvements: first, in the appearance of the furniture; secondly, in the elimination of the front legs of the chair...and thirdly, in the simplification of the manufacturing process. I have made one model chair. The system works, and I am trying to organize the necessary development work with the aluminium industry." (Letter 13 Sept. 1946, Pritchard Archive, University of Newcastle-upon-Tyne.)

78. Undated manuscript, "Draft (of) History of the Isokon Furniture Company," Pritchard Archive.

79. Memorandum written by Pritchard, Pritchard Archive.

80. "Draft History...," Pritchard Archive.

81. Memorandum, Pritchard Archive.

82. English patent, "Improvements in Chairs" (478,138), filed 10 July 1936.

83. English patent, "Improvements in Chairs, Tables, Stools, and like pieces of Furniture" (479,529), filed 12 Aug. 1936.

84. The English distributors of Aalto furniture, Finmar Ltd, found the Breuer chair all too similar to Aalto's designs; in July 1936 they accused Breuer of infringing on Aalto's patent. Breuer replied that he could not "see any similarity between this design [Aalto's] and my own...I do not see any reason for stopping

the manufacture of my design." (Pritchard Archive.) Negotiations between Pritchard (Breuer's representative for plywood furniture) and Artek (the Finnish manufacturer of Aalto furniture) ensued, and eventually involved Moholy-Nagy and Morton Shand. By June 1937, Pritchard, on advice of counsel, agreed to a licensing agreement that would recognize the Aalto design but would not require Breuer to pay any substantial royalty. Both sides agreed to "keep off the designs of the other." (Pritchard Archive.) The agreement, however, was never signed after Pritchard found an illustration of the Aalto chair published before the date of the English patent.

85. "A Remodelled Interior at Clifton," *Architectural Review*, vol. 13, no. 79 (Mar. 1936), p. 140.

86. Marcel Breuer, "A House at Bristol," *Design for Today*, vol. 3 (Dec. 1935), p. 459.

87. Ibid.

88. The decision was made by a committee of students, alumnae, and the school's Director of Halls.

89. "House in Pittsburgh, Pa.," *Architectural Forum*, vol. 74 (Mar. 1941), p. 160.

90. James Ford and Katherine Morrow Ford, *Design of Modern Interiors* (New York: Architectural Book Publishing Co., 1942), p. 116.

91. "House in Pittsburgh, Pa.," p. 160.

92. Ford and Ford, p. 116.

93. "Project for a Workers House," *California Arts & Architecture* (Dec. 1943), p. 24.

94. Much of the detailed information in this section comes from "The Resilient Chair," an unpublished booklet handed in with Breuer's competition entry as a report on the research project.

95. Letter from Breuer to Pritchard, 13 Sept. 1946, Pritchard Archive.

96. "The Resilient Chair," p. 9.

97. Ibid.

98. In 1957, Marcel Breuer and Associates was formed and later became a partnership between Breuer, Herbert Beckhard, Murray Emslie, Robert F. Gatje, and Hamilton P. Smith. The firm continues in existence today.

99. "The Resilient Chair," pp. 22–23.

BIBLIOGRAPHY

An extensive bibliography on Breuer's career up to 1949, prepared by Hannah B. Muller, appeared in Peter Blake's monograph. The present bibliography lists recently assembled collections of primary material that have provided the bulk of the information for this book. Important publications not listed in Blake as well as those that have appeared since 1949 are also noted below.

PRIMARY SOURCES

1. Marcel Breuer Collection, George Arents Research Library for Special Collections, Syracuse University. Contains virtually all of Breuer's surviving correspondence, bills, contracts, specifications, drawings, and photographs up to 1951. Earliest original items are from 1926. There is much correspondence from 1931–37, but the major portion of the collection is from Breuer's years in the U.S.
2. Pritchard Archive, University of Newcastle-upon-Tyne, England. The most complete collection of Isokon material. Extensive correspondence with Breuer, although additional Isokon material is to be found in the Marcel Breuer Collection. Included are Breuer and other Isokon drawings.
3. Papers of Anton Lorenz, owned by Peter Fletcher, Boynton Beach, Fla. Correspondence, patents, drawings, and other documentary material on Lorenz' career.
4. Thonet Archive, Thonet Industries, York, Pa. Includes all Thonet tubular-steel catalogs with Breuer furniture and the only known copy of Breuer's first design registration.

SECONDARY SOURCES

Argan, Giulio Carlo. *Marcel Breuer disegno industriale e architettura.* Milan: Görlich Editore, 1957.

Banham, Reyner. *Theory and Design in the First Machine Age.* New York: Praeger, 1970.

Bann, Stephen, ed. *The Tradition of Constructivism.* New York: Viking, 1974.

Baroni, Daniele. *The Furniture of Gerrit Thomas Rietveld.* Woodbury, N.Y.: Barron's, 1978.

Bayer, Herbert, and Gropius, Walter and Ise. *Bauhaus 1919–1928.* New York: The Museum of Modern Art, 1938.

Benton, Tim and Charlotte, with Sharp, Dennis. *Architecture and Design 1890–1939.* New York: Whitney Library of Design, 1975.

Blake, Peter. *Marcel Breuer, Architect and Designer.* New York: The Museum of Modern Art, 1949.

——————, ed. *Marcel Breuer: Sun and Shadow.* New York: Dodd, Mead & Co., 1955.

Breuer, Marcel. "Genesis of Design," in Gyorgy Kepes, ed., *The Man-Made Object.* New York: George Braziller, 1966.

——————. "A House at Bristol," *Design for Today,* vol. 3 (Dec. 1935), pp. 459–62.

——————. Statement on his own work in "8 Architects on Exhibition" *Trend in Design of Everyday Things,* vol. 1, no. 2 (Summer 1936), pp. 108–13.

——————. "Project for a Workers House" (reprinted as "On a Binuclear House"), *California Arts & Architecture* (Dec. 1943), pp. 24–25.

Brown, Theodore M. *The Work of G. Rietveld, Architect.* Utrecht: Bruna & Zoon, 1958.

Designed by 7 Architects. Foreword by E. Maxwell Fry. London: Heal & Son, 1936.

Eckstein, Hans. *Die Schöne Wohnung.* Munich: F. Bruckmann, 1934.

50 Years Bauhaus. Toronto: Art Gallery of Ontario, 1969.

form + zweck, vol. 11, no. 3 (1979), special Bauhaus issue.

Franciscono, Marcel. *Walter Gropius and the Creation of the Bauhaus in Weimar.* Urbana: University of Illinois Press, 1971.

Geest, Jan van, and Mácel, Otakar. *Stühle aus Stahl.* Cologne: König, 1980.

Glaeser, Ludwig. *Ludwig Mies van der Rohe, Furniture and Furniture Drawings.* New York: The Museum of Modern Art, 1977.

Grieve, Alastair. *Isokon Exhibition.* [Norwich]: University of East Anglia, 1975.

Hassenpflug, Gustav. "Mobel aus Stahlrohr und Stahlblech," special issue of *Stahl Uberall,* vol. 9, no. 5 (1936).

——————. *Stahlmöbel.* Düsseldorf: Verlag Stahl-iesen, 1960.

Hoffmann, Herbert. *Intérieurs Modernes.* Paris: Librairie Gründ, 1930.

Hüter, Karl-Heinz. *Das Bauhaus in Weimar.* Berlin: Akademie Verlag, 1976.

Jordy, William. "Aftermath of the Bauhaus: Mies, Gropius, and Breuer," *Perspectives in American History,* vol. 2 (1968), pp. 485–543.

——————. *American Buildings and Their Architects,* vol. 4, *The Impact of European Modernism in* the Mid-Twentieth Century. Garden City, N.Y.: Anchor Press/Doubleday, 1976.

Kaufmann, Edgar, Jr. Prize Designs for Modern Furniture. New York: The Museum of Modern Art, 1950.

Le Corbusier. Towards a New Architecture. New York: Praeger, 1972.

Logie, Gordon. Furniture from Machines. London: Allen & Unwin, 1947.

Marcel Breuer. New York: Metropolitan Museum of Art, 1972.

Marcel Breuer: Architektur, Möbel, Design. Berlin: Bauhaus Archiv, 1975.

Marcel Breuer: Buildings and Projects 1921–1961. Introduction by Cranston Jones. New York: Praeger, 1962.

"Metal Chairs," Architectural Record, vol. 68, no. 3 (Sept. 1930), pp. 209–14.

Metalen Buisstoelen 1925–1940. Delft: Stedelijk Museum 'Het Prinsenhof,' 1975.

Müller-Wulckow, Walter. Deutsche Wohnung der Gegenwart. Königstein: Karl Robert Langeweische Verlag, 1931.

Papachristou, Tician. Marcel Breuer: New Buildings and Projects. New York: Praeger, 1970.

Platz, Gustav. Wohnräume der Gegenwart. Berlin: Propyläen Verlag, 1933.

Robinson, Heath, and Browne, K. R. G. How to Live in a Flat. London: Hutchinson & Co., 1936.

Scheidig, Walter. The Crafts of the Bauhaus Weimar. London: Studio Vista, [1966].

Schneck, Adolf. Der Stuhl. Stuttgart: Julius Hoffmann, 1937.

Scully, Vincent. "Doldrums in the Suburbs," Perspecta, 9/10 (1965), pp. 281–90.

Seeger, Mia. Der neue Wohnbedarf. Stuttgart: Julius Hoffmann, 1931.

Sharp, Dennis; Benton, Tim; and Cole, Barbie Campbell. Pel and Tubular Steel Furniture of the Thirties. London: Architectural Association, 1977.

Spiegel, Hans. Der Stahlhausbau, 1., Wohnbauten aus Stahl. Leipzig: Alwin Fröhlich Verlag, 1928.

Typenmöbel. Basel: Gewerbemuseum, 1929.

Wilk, Christopher. Thonet: 150 years of Furniture. Woodbury, N.Y.: Barron's, 1980.

Willet, John. The New Sobriety: Art and Politics in the Weimar Period, 1917–1933. London: Thames and Hudson, 1978.

Wingler, Hans M. The Bauhaus. Cambridge, Mass.: M.I.T. Press, 1976.

PHOTOGRAPHIC CREDITS

The numbers listed below refer to figures.

Architectural Press, London: 136, 139, 140, 147–49.

Bauhaus Archiv, Berlin: 2, 20, 22, 24, 47, 52.

Marcel Breuer Associates, New York: frontispiece, 105, 106, 112, 150, 167, 179, 190, 192.

Marcel Breuer Collection, George Arents Research Library for Special Collections, Syracuse University: 65, 117.

Thomas Breuer: 187.

The Brooklyn Museum: 73.

Bryn Mawr College (Karl Dimler): 155.

Busch-Reisinger Museum, Harvard University: 165, 186.

Richard Cheek, Belmont, Mass.: 91, 92.

City Museum and Art Gallery, Bristol, England: 125.

Robert Damora, New Canaan: 177.

Paul Davis, George H. Davis Studio, Boston: 152.

Peter Fletcher, Boynton Beach, Fla.: 118.

Reinhard Friedrich, Berlin: 50, 77, 119.

P. E. Guerrero, New Canaan: 178, 180, 189.

Hutchinson & Co., Ltd, London: 63.

Shin Koyama, Bloomington, Minn.: 188.

Hans Kruse, Delft, Netherlands: 122.

Musée des Arts Décoratifs, Paris: 33.

The Museum of Modern Art, New York: 1, 3–6, 7 (G. Barrows), 8 (V. Parker), 9 (K. Keller), 10–19, 21, 23, 25 (V. Parker), 26–30, 31 (G. Barrows), 32, 34–46, 48, 49, 51 (K. Keller), 53–62, 64, 66 (V. Parker), 67, 68 (K. Keller), 69, 70, 71 (V. Parker), 72 (K. Keller), 74–76, 78 (M. Olatunji), 79–90, 93–104, 107–11, 113–16, 120, 121 (V. Parker), 123, 126 (G. Barrows), 127, 129, 131 (G. Barrows), 132, 133, 135 (M. Olatunji), 137, 138, 141–45, 151, 163, 164, 170, 172 (K. Keller), 173, 174, 194–99.

New York Public Library, Research Division: 136.

Pritchard Archive, University of Newcastle-upon-Tyne: 124.

Warren Reynolds, Minneapolis: 182.

Royal Institute of British Architects, London: 146.

Ben Schnall, courtesy Marcel Breuer Associates: 180, 181, 183–85, 191.

Sotheby's, London: 128.

Ezra Stoller, Esto, Mamaroneck, N.Y.: 153, 154, 156–62, 166, 168, 169, 171, 175, 176.

Thonet Archive, Thonet Industries, York, Pa.: 193.

Victoria and Albert Museum, London: 130, 134.